ERIK GUNNAR ASPLUND

Taking an interdisciplinary approach, weaving together art, philosophy, history, and literature, this book investigates the landscapes and buildings of Swedish architect Erik Gunnar Asplund. Through critical essays and beautiful illustrations focusing on four projects, the Woodland Cemetery, the Stockholm Public Library, the Stockholm Exhibition and Asplund's own house at Stennäs, it addresses the topic of buildings accompanied by landscapes.

It proposes that themes related to landscape are central to Asplund's distinctive work, with these particular sites forming a collection that documents an evolution in his design thinking from 1915 to 1940. The architect himself wrote comparatively little about his design intentions. However, through close reading and analysis of the selected projects as landscapes with architecture, author Malcolm Woollen argues that reflections of the history of Swedish landscape architecture and the intellectual climate in the late nineteenth and early twentieth centuries are evident in his work and help to explain the architect's intentions.

This book is a must-have for academics, advanced students and researchers in landscape architecture and design who are interested in Nordic Classicism and the works of Erik Gunnar Asplund.

Malcolm Woollen is an architect and an Assistant Visiting Professor at Pennsylvania State University, USA.

ERIK GUNNAR ASPLUND

Landscapes and Buildings

Malcolm Woollen

Routledge
Taylor & Francis Group
LONDON AND NEW YORK

First published 2019
by Routledge
2 Park Square, Milton Park, Abingdon, Oxon OX14 4RN

and by Routledge
711 Third Avenue, New York, NY 10017

Routledge is an imprint of the Taylor & Francis Group, an informa business

British Library Cataloguing-in-Publication Data
A catalogue record for this book is available from the British Library

Library of Congress Cataloging-in-Publication Data
Names: Woollen, Malcolm, author.
Title: Erik Gunnar Asplund : landscapes and buildings / Malcolm Woollen.
Description: New York : Routledge, 2018. | Includes bibliographical references and index.
Identifiers: LCCN 2018003461| ISBN 9780815378211 (hardback) | ISBN 9780815378228 (pbk.) | ISBN 9781351232999 (ebook)
Subjects: LCSH: Asplund, Erik Gunnar, 1885-1940—Criticism and interpretation.
Classification: LCC NA1293.A77 W66 2018 | DDC 720.92—dc23
LC record available at https://lccn.loc.gov/2018003461

ISBN: 978-0-8153-7821-1 (hbk)
ISBN: 978-0-8153-7822-8 (pbk)
ISBN: 978-1-351-23299-9 (ebk)

Typeset in Bembo and Stone Sans
by Florence Production Ltd, Stoodleigh, Devon, UK

To John Dixon Hunt
for his inspiration, encouragement, and critique

CONTENTS

ILLUSTRATIONS

PREFACE

This is not a monograph on Asplund's complete works. That need has been met admirably in books by Peter Blundell Jones and Stuart Wrede.[1] Instead, it attempts to address the topic of landscapes with buildings through critical essays on four projects: the Woodland Cemetery, the Stockholm Public Library (or Stadsbiblioteket), the Stockholm Exhibition, and Asplund's own house at Stennäs. This is not to claim that other projects by Asplund do not use landscape in interesting ways. Instead, it proposes that themes related to landscape are central to Asplund's work and that these particular works form a collection that touches on all aspects of public and private life and documents an evolution in his thinking from 1915 to 1940.

Other scholars have treated this subject in different ways over the last thirty years. Caroline Constant has thoroughly documented the landscape and architecture of the Woodland Cemetery and written an article about Observatorielunden and the Stadsbibliotek.[2] In addition to his monograph, Stuart Wrede has also contributed an article on Asplund's landscapes.[3] As a caveat, this book is not based on any new archival discoveries. Instead, it relies on existing monographs to explain essential background information. What distinguishes this study is a close reading of the selected sites as landscapes *with* architecture. This is an interdisciplinary challenge that has been largely unmet by existing scholarship. To achieve this, it is intended to expand upon existing research in three ways. One is to attempt a consideration of the cultural climate of the period in relation to Asplund's landscapes and buildings. Another is to place Asplund in the context of the history of landscape architecture in Sweden. A third is to use comparative analysis to arrive at concepts that develop in more than one project.

This agenda is more difficult because Asplund's thinking shifted from National Romanticism to Neoclassicism and then to Functionalism. This swift transition mirrors a rapid change in Sweden in the early twentieth century from a Nordic backwater to a modern socialist state. As a further complication, Asplund wrote very little about his artistic motivations. His accounts of his work in *Byggmästaren*, the Swedish architectural journal of the time, are perfunctory, and a list of books in his library does not survive. Even as a professor of architecture, he was very reticent about his own artistic agenda and sources of inspiration. From accounts of colleagues and employees, it is apparent that they, too, did not fully understand his intentions.[4] In addition, in all the projects under consideration here, there are gestures that resist one clear explanation. As a result, it is hard to escape the conclusion that deliberate ambiguity was his aim; he wanted his legacy to be about an individual reading of landscapes and buildings, unencumbered by any particular written agenda or doctrine on his part.

It might be said that this book runs the risk of breaking the spell cast by this ambiguity and encouraging one doctrine. On the contrary, it is intended to draw attention to this ambiguity and reveal possible interpretations, rather than limit them. As part of his practice of ambiguity, Asplund wished to situate the visitor in a psychological space between individuality, Swedish cultural legacy, and the natural world. This kind of appreciation, with all of its required cultural background, is difficult enough for Swedes and even more difficult for a foreigner. It is the purpose of this book to help the reader to arrive at a higher level of understanding and to demonstrate that landscape was the critical component of this ambiguous agenda.

Another consideration, beyond the appreciation of ambiguity, is the accumulated learning that allows one project to contribute to the next. It is a misconception to think that all architects find their beliefs afresh before any building takes form. It is closer to the truth to state that, while many architects seek out certain projects, the resolution of those projects, including the interaction with clients, leaves a profound imprint on their thinking. The Woodland Cemetery, a comprehensive landscape project, was the beginning point for Asplund. He brings some of that sensibility to large projects that follow, including the Stadsbibliotek and the Stockholm Exhibition, where invaluable lessons were learned about what fails and what works and the role of landscape in modern programs. In particular, this book tells the story of the failure of his version of the Neoclassical landscape and the development of a modern approach to landscape that was intimately connected to his version of Functionalist architecture. The story ends at the time of Asplund's death in 1940, when he had succeeded, with Lewerentz's collaboration, in finishing the Woodland Cemetery by using his new understanding of modern landscape and Functionalist architecture, derived from the Stadsbibliotek and the Stockholm Exhibition. A practice that began by defining an expression of one particular national landscape ended by clarifying a new one, equally potent.

Notes

1 See Peter Blundell Jones, *Gunnar Asplund* (London: Phaidon Press, 2006) and Stuart Wrede, *The Architecture of Erik Gunnar Asplund* (Cambridge, MA: MIT Press, 1980).

2 See Caroline Constant, *The Woodland Cemetery: Toward a Spiritual Landscape* (Stockholm, Sweden: Byggförlaget, 1994) and Caroline Constant, "The Stockholm Public Library: Architecture between Nature and City," *Arquitectura* 280, no. 5 (1989): 54–67.

3 See Stuart Wrede, "Landscape and Architecture: The Work of Erik Gunnar Asplund," *Perspecta* 20 (1983): 195–214.

4 See Christina Engfors, Ed., *E. G. Asplund, Architect, Friend and Colleague* (Stockholm, Sweden: Arikitektur Förlag, 1990).

ACKNOWLEDGEMENTS

The following individuals have contributed in small and large ways to this project; Jerome Singerman of Penn Press for his kindness and support; Stuart Wrede and Shayne O'Neil for helpful comments and insight; Nicklas Edell, Javier Beltran, and Göran Berselius of the Stockholm Cemetery Administration for answering many questions; Hedvig Schönbäck of the Stockholm City Museum for providing background on the Woodland Chapel; Eva Eriksson, Eva Rudberg, and Caroline Constant, all distinguished historians, for answering endless small questions related to history and images; Ewa Andersson for an informative tour of the Stadsbibliotek; Annika Tengstrand and Johan Örn of the Swedish Center for Architecture and Design for patient help over many years; Wendy Adams, Terry Schiavone, and Tim Auman of Penn State Libraries for help with images and interlibrary loans; Arne Wittstrand for his help with Erik Bülow Hübe's contribution to the Stockholm Exhibition; Ulrika Strömquist of the National Library of Sweden for extraordinary attention and care; Catrin Lundeberg and Lars Engelhardt of Prins Eugens Waldemarsudde for their kindness; Berit Schütz and Olle Norling of Upplandsmuseet for their persistence and generosity; Jonas Hedberg of the Nordic Museum for dealing with unsual requests; Fiffi Myrström of Böhuslansmuseet, Anita Christiansen of Svensk Form and Eva-Lena Bengtson of Konstakademien for prompt attention with images; Gary Backhaus and Troy Paddock of IASESP for publishing an article on the Stockholm Exhibition; Anne T. Demo for supporting and publishing early research on the Woodland Cemetery; Aoife McGrath and Grace Harrison of Routledge for their good judgment and care; the Hagerud family for their hospitality at Stennäs; Tove Falk for her beautiful photographs and tour of Stockholm; Colin St. John Wilson for an early introduction to Asplund's works; Evans Woollen for his financial and moral support; Christine Gorby for her thoughtful advice and forbearance.

1

INTRODUCTION

Asplund's distinctive contribution lies in his use of landscape architecture with architecture. It would be a mistake, however, to view this in isolation and regard it as his innovation completely. It would also be careless to overlook the importance of landscape in Swedish culture and the development of traditions in landscape architecture. Finally, the significant schools of thought in the first decades of the twentieth century, in both design and painting, should not be neglected. Though discussion of all of these subjects is offered throughout this book, this introduction is intended to offer essential background for those who come to this subject for the first time.

Through the nineteenth and early twentieth centuries, Sweden established a new identity that was distinctive in Western Europe. This was a process that was prompted by different crises that redirected attention to the most important national priorities. First, there was the loss of Finland in 1809, a traditional part of Sweden since the Middle Ages. In reaction to this event, Esaias Tegnér wrote, "Weep Svea for what you have lost; but protect what you have . . . [W]ithin Sweden's borders win Finland once again" (Barton 2005, 318). One of the most productive responses to this appeal was to found a nationalism that "drew less upon history than upon the quiet beauties of the Swedish landscape and Sweden's ancient folk culture" (319). This was again the departure point when there was a national discussion after Norway renounced the union with Sweden in 1905. Ellen Key, an intellectual engaged in social reform, wished at the time to find new purpose in "the true Swedish sentiment," which was "the deep, shy, taciturn, modest love of (our) homeland, the earth-bound feeling for our forest-scented home place" (320). On both occasions, the prevailing response was an introspective appreciation of the landscape of the home country associated with reflection on what Sweden should be in the future.

It is important to bear this history in mind as landscape architecture moves from the exclusive domain of the aristocracy in the nineteenth century to become a popular form. Particularly beginning in the late nineteenth century, new social agendas and priorities were expressed through an affiliation with landscape. Asplund's achievement was to recognize this reality and to escape the possibility of deadening conformity associated with nationalist themes. In this respect, he showed how the Swedish condition could be reinterpreted through the classical tradition and later through Functionalist thinking from abroad. In addition to opening a national preoccupation with landscape to other influences, he also demonstrated that a progressive conception of Sweden could be understood through landscape by inviting *active* imagination. In effect, you could be Swedish not only by taking pleasure in the sensual and reaffirming qualities of landscape but also through reflecting on poetic associations between culture, human bodies, and the natural world.

While modern landscape architecture in Sweden became more responsive to the place, it was more faithful to foreign models in earlier periods. In particular, during the seventeenth and eighteenth centuries, the influence was French. Nicodemus Tessin the Younger, the court architect from 1681 to 1728, learned the art of landscape architecture through an association with Le Nôtre and a very close reading of A. J. Dézallier d'Argenville's *Le Theorie et la practique du jardinage* (Olausson 1997, 267). His most significant commission was the design for the gardens of Drottingholm Palace, located to the west of Stockholm, beginning in 1680 (Figure 1.1). Though Tessin was faithful to a fault to his French examples, he still faced the problem of adapting the French parterre garden to the Swedish landscape and climate; he was creative through necessity, not through any gift of imagination. Repeated blasting was required to adequately prepare the landscape for the axial garden. When a particular outcrop resisted all attempts at blasting, Tessin decided that an edifice with a cascade over the natural rock was the best solution (271). Though French gardens of the period invariably had fountains and canals, Tessin prudently chose to omit them entirely from the project. Though he practiced in the French manner for his public projects, his own private garden was Italian in inspiration. Called a *locus ameonus*, this was a modest place of refuge with "box hedge patterns, trimmed bushes and urns" as well as "a nympheum with a pair of sculptures of Greek philosophers." Here he sought an illusion of a larger space with frescoes of landscapes, analogous to those of Claude Lorrain or Poussin (Karling 1981, 13).

Following Tessin's death, leadership in landscape architecture in the early eighteenth century passed to Carl Hårleman. He practiced in an updated Rococo style that made some accommodation to the larger natural environment. Grass patterns were used for parterres; some rocky areas were treated artfully instead of being erased, and kitchen gardens were treated with some prominence (Karling 1981, 17). At Ulriksdal, he even created a small "natural park" at the south edge of the parterre. "This is an early, indeed the very earliest instance of natural scenery immediately adjoining a pleasure park in Sweden" (18). Another novel

FIGURE 1.1 View of the Drottningholm Palace Gardens, Nicodemus Tessin the Younger, 1680–1728

Source: Gustav Heurlin photo, Västergötlandsmuseet, 1M16-B63630075

device used by Hårleman was the "look-out point," used at Stola Manor, "marked by memorial stones, on a hill in the immediate vicinity of the manor" (19). Magnus Gabriel de la Gardie had also designed one at Ulriksdal with "Italian style temple-like edifices." At Rosersberg in Uppland, Bengt Oxenstierna gave the idea a Nordic emphasis by redesigning the top of a prehistoric burial mound with rune stones and an arrangement of conifers (19).

After Hårleman's death in 1753, Swedish landscape architecture languished under the leadership of Carl Fredrik Adelcrantz, who departed from the Rococo in favor of a more austere classical manner. This trend changed with the beginning of the reign of Gustav III in 1766. The young king had been educated in the fine arts and landscape architecture by Tessin's son Carl Gustaf. In particular, he had been encouraged to take an interest in Italian gardens and the English Picturesque (Olausson 1997, 272). When the young king made it clear that he wanted a garden in the English manner built on the marshy ground to the north of Tessin's Drottingholm garden, Adelcrantz knew that he was not up to the task. He advised the king to support Fredrik Magnus Piper, a young architect, in his studies of gardens in England and Italy, with the expectation that he would have the necessary skill and imagination to undertake the king's project. As Magnus Olausson makes clear, Piper's career marked a turning point in the history of Swedish landscape architecture because he could work imaginatively within an international style without the slavish eclecticism of his predecessors, despite the king's requests for some direct references to examples in Italy and England (276).

During Piper's time in England, he made a lengthy study of Stourhead, in particular, documenting all aspects of the garden. He also worked for a period with William Chambers, the architect of the improvements at Kew and author of

A Dissertation on Oriental Gardening.[1] Chambers wished to distinguish himself from the approach of Capability Brown by advocating a greater role for art and imagination. "Where twining serpentine walks, scattering shrubs, digging holes to raise mole-hills and ringing never-ceasing changes on lawns, groves and thickets, is called Gardening, it matters little who are the Gardeners" (Hunt and Willis 1993, 322). Through his experience of Chinese gardens, he found that, though their artists have "nature for their model, yet they are not so attached to her as to exclude all appearance of art" (Chambers 1773, 13).

> The Chinese are therefore no enemies to straight lines: because they are, generally speaking, productive of grandeur, which often cannot be attained without them: nor have they any aversion to regular geometric figures, which they say are beautiful in themselves, and well suited to small compositions, where the luxuriant irregularities of nature would fill up and embarrass the parts they should adorn.
>
> (Chambers 1773, 14)

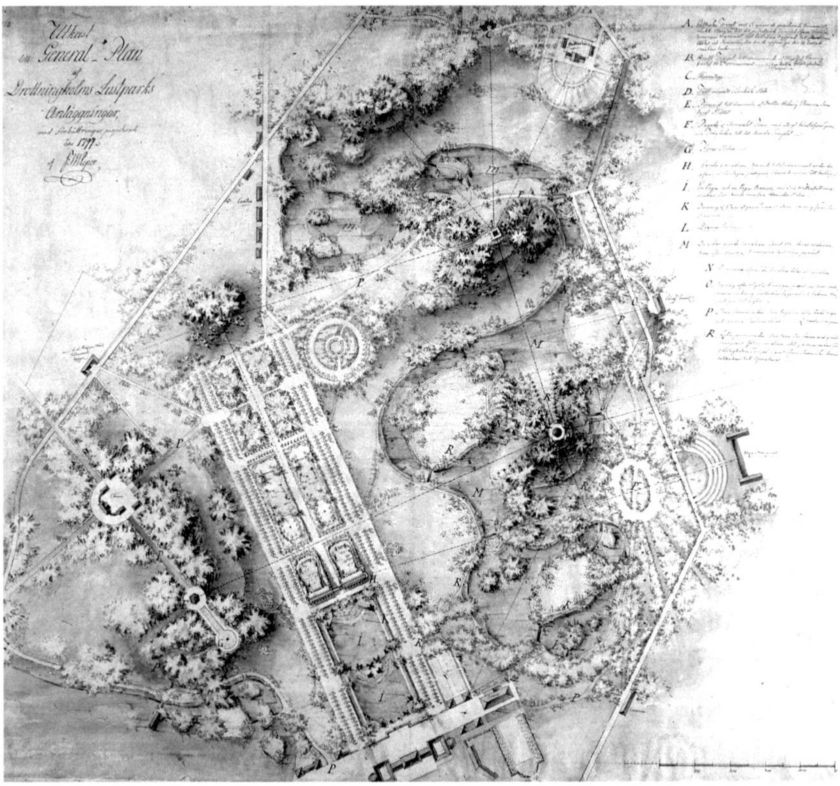

FIGURE 1.2 Plan of Drottningholm Palace Gardens, Fredrick Magnus Piper, 1797

Source: Konstakademien

Chambers goes on to explain that neither too great an adherence to nature nor artfulness is appropriate. "One manner is absurd; the other insipid and vulgar: a judicious mixture of both would certainly be more perfect than either" (viii).

It is possible to see a realization of Chambers's dictum in the superimposition of lines of radiating lime trees over a meandering canal and an island at Gustav III's picturesque park at Drottingholm (Figure 1.2). One kind of artifice related to making multiple view corridors of the mound on the island has been overlaid on another related to the manipulation of the canals in a picturesque way. A viewer circulating around the island enjoys the repetitive framed *inward* views of the mound and multiple *outward* views of different objects in a picturesque landscape. A monumental statement of landscape architecture, a role usually taken by a building, becomes the element that asserts hierarchy and organizes the experience of the garden.

The pleasure garden at Haga, also commissioned by Gustav III, is different and less obvious as an exemplar of Chambers's principles.[2] "The Great Pelouse," a grand bowl-like lawn that slopes towards the Brunnsviken, is the organizing space of the garden (Figure 1.3). Assorted pavilions of exotic design have been placed at oblique angles so none commands the lawn exclusively (Figure 1.4). Buildings of a larger scale, such as Gustav III 's unfinished Great Palace and Haga Slott, have been concealed in the woodland. Of the many pavilions, those with the pride of place are the Cooper Tents, designed by L. J. Desprez in 1787 (Figure 1.5). These extraordinary structures would later draw the attention of Asplund and fellow Neoclassicists more than one hundred years later and become a reference point for buildings at the Stockholm Exhibition and the Woodland Cemetery.

Karling notes that Piper was also involved with modifications to Kungsträdgården, near the palace in Stockholm, as well as Logården. These were efforts to make the gardens more accessible to people from all classes. "In this way Piper opened the way for the social breakthrough in landscape design which can be said to have come with the development of town parks in the nineteenth century" (Karling 1981, 35). These town parks were created as part of a larger movement called National Romanticism that had its roots among classical scholars in the early nineteenth century. Among these authors, Erik Gustaf Geijer (1783–1847), a poet, composer, historian, philosopher, and politician, was the most significant figure. In his *History of the Swedish People*, he consciously writes of the Baltic as a northern version of the Mediterranean and Sweden as a cradle of Baltic civilization, analogous to Greece (Geijer 1845, 3). He also did not fail to note the common traits between Norse and Greek mythology and "the principle of tragic irony which pervades the whole mythical scheme" (6). Geijer made an even more significant contribution as the founder of the Gothic Society, named after the people who inhabited Sweden originally. This was a group of intellectuals who campaigned for a broad cultural revival based on history, folktales, poetry, and songs. "Its imperative, cultural, not political, was to preserve Sweden's ethnic heritage, highlighting cultural similarities that transcended regional identity and social class" (Facos 1998, 32).

FIGURE 1.3
The "Great Pelouse," Haga Park, Fredrick Magnus Piper, 1781–87

Source: Peter Isotalo photo, 2007

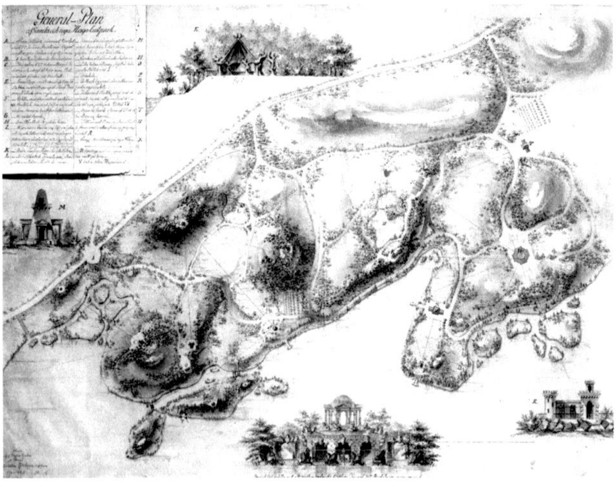

FIGURE 1.4
Haga Park site plan, Fredrik Magnus Piper, 1781

Source: Broschyren "Hagapromenader"

FIGURE 1.5
Copper Tents, Haga Park, Jean Louis Desprez, Solna, 1787

Source: Gustav Heurlin photo, 1924, Västergötlandsmuseet, 1M16-B63625074

The other leading member of the Gothic Society was the aforementioned Esaias Tegnér (1782–1846), the most celebrated Swedish poet of the nineteenth century and author of *Frithjof's Saga*, a monumental work composed in twenty-four cantos of different verse forms.[3] Roughly based on an Icelandic saga, it tells the story of a young Viking warrior who is exiled after burning down a temple. During his time away, he travels to the Greek islands and learns to appreciate Greek culture. On his return, he rebuilds the temple with a colonnade and learns to moderate his violent emotions. Many of these cantos were arranged as songs and were sung by schoolchildren well into the twentieth century (Nolin 1996, 190).

The leaders of the Gothic Society assumed important positions as prelates, professors, and politicians. As Facos relates, they achieved the curricular reforms that created the National Romantic consciousness in Sweden (Facos 1998, 33). Geijer expresses their idea of a people unified by the past and creating the future with the past in the following passage: "Every folk lives not only in the present, but also in its memories: and it lives *through* them. Every generation propagates itself both physically and morally, bequeathing to the next generation its customs and its concepts. This tradition that continues from one time to another unifies a people, fostering their unbroken consciousness of themselves as a nation: it transmits to them, so to speak, their personality" (Facos 1998, 34).

The work of the Gothic Society was an inspiration for many literary works in the mid-nineteenth century. Its reflection in landscape architecture is only seen late in the century with the development of new urban parks, mentioned earlier. Among the more celebrated of these were Slottskogen in Göteborg and the Municipal Park in Jönköping (Figure 1.6). Both are regarded as "nature" parks created in response to articles from the 1870s that advocated for parks that would be made from existing landscapes without the use of imported styles (Nolin 2004, 198).[4] Formerly, workers had sought weekend entertainment in the nearby countryside, while the bourgeoisie used existing parks for promenades. These parks were intended to be open to all, with fewer restrictions about appropriate pathways (200). In particular, they also served the agenda of the Temperance movement, presenting more options for leisure than congregating at the local pub. After opening, both parks acted as vehicle for social policies. Children had a venue for athletics, including skiiing, sledding, running, and bicycling. Teachers took advantage of a new laboratory for education in the natural sciences (202–03). Later, at Jönköping, antiquarians succeeded in opening an open-air museum within the park with reconstructed houses and native animals, analogous to Skansen in Stockholm (207).

While these parks were intended to offer working people a place of leisure, political gatherings were strictly forbidden (Nolin 2004, 202). This was in response to growing political unrest and the rise of the Social Democrats in the late nineteenth century. Emigration to the United States was on the rise, forcing a new awareness of the limited opportunities and injustices of rural life. Workers in urban industries, meanwhile, had limited rights, oppressive conditions, and poor housing.

FIGURE 1.6 Slottskogen, Swan Pond, Göteborg, 1880–90

Source: Alfred Andersson photo, 1920, Bohusläns Museum, UMFA53202 0411

Those on the left were campaigning for a new consensus that required both swift modernization and a more equitable society to keep Swedes from leaving. While shared by many, these aims were explicitly promoted by the Social Democratic Party (SPD). Partly in response to their exclusion from public places, the party formed the *folkets* park and the *folkhus*, a form of union hall, which were constructed in small cities all over Sweden. Some of these parks were modeled after amusement parks, whereas others attempted to preserve outcrops and forests while developing outdoor performance spaces (Ståhl 2005).

At this time art and politics were closely associated through the efforts of National Romantic painters who had returned to Sweden in the 1880s after long stays in Paris, newly committed to shaping national consciousness through art. Initially, while in exile, these artists called themselves the Opponents, but they reconstituted themselves as the Artists' Association in 1886 (Facos 1998, 23). Significant painters included Richard Bergh, Prince Eugen, Bruno Liljefors, Anders Zorn, Carl Larsson, and Karl Nordström. Over nearly three decades these painters, among others, produced paintings of Swedish landscapes that attempt to express emotional qualities inherent in clouds, land forms, sea, and forests. Other favorite subjects included the human body within nature, the relationship of typical Swedish buildings to equally familiar landscapes, and colorful folklife. Because their works reflected popular themes, reproductions of works by these painters appeared in textbooks, as affordable prints, and in public buildings (Nolin 2013, 123).[5] "National Romantic painting triumphed because it mirrored the aspirations of its generation and because a network of powerful politicians, collectors and writers promoted it" (181).

In the early twentieth century, the ideals of National Romanticism were sustained in monumental architectural projects that related more closely with landscape than with an urban order. Ragnar Östberg designed a new Town Hall for Stockholm in a grandiose version of Swedish vernacular that favors a relationship with Lake Mälaren. Lars Israel Wahlman conceived of St. Engelbrekt's Church in Stockholm as a soaring form that completes the top of a steep outcrop.[6] Ivar Tengbom's Högalids Church (1917–23) also commands a high point in Stockholm with two attenuated towers (Figure 1.7). In addition to his noteworthy church projects, Wahlman was also the architect for numerous country houses and gardens.[7] These reveal his commitment to English Arts and Crafts ideals and a conviction that an architect should take responsibility for gardens, regarding them as an extension of a dwelling and a suitable place for repose. Like those who invented the "nature park" in the late nineteenth century, he rejected the use of flower beds and favored native species above all (Nolin 2008, 195). These attitudes were widely shared in the early twentieth century, promoted in books by Rudolf Abelin that instructed homeowners about the art of domestic gardening.[8]

As a departure from National Romantic orthodoxy, Neoclassicism briefly became the prevailing style among Swedish architects in the second decade of the twentieth century. The sources for this new movement were diverse. Some younger architects were interested in work that was happening in Germany at the time, while others took inspiration from a German book entitled *Um 1800* by Paul Mebes.[9] Works in Denmark by Hack Kampmann, C. L. Hanson, and Andreas Kirkerup also commanded attention.[10] Even more significant was that young Swedish architects, including Asplund and Ivar Tengbom, made their version of the Grand Tour, where they took pleasure in commonplace urbanism. It is even more noteworthy that they took particular interest in Greek temples as part of larger landscapes.

While Neoclassical architecture in Sweden is quite distinctive, it should not be seen as a complete departure from the ideals of National Romanticism. Asplund, Tengbom, Lewerentz, and their colleagues sought new forms of monumentality, but they also wished to sustain particular Swedish qualities. Proportions tend to be attenuated, making columns notably taller relative to their width. Materials were generally inexpensive, rarely departing from colored stucco, the standard choice for Stockholm buildings. Despite the monumental status of certain buildings, architects also wished to relate them to more everyday activity and the natural world. Tengbom's Concert Hall in Stockholm, for example, has shops that face Sveavägen, and the front entrance is oriented towards Hötorget, a market square (Figure 1.8). While this location enhanced the view of his building, he also wished that the noise and view of the market should be part of the experience of his building. Asplund, likewise, preserved a marketplace behind the Stadsbibliotek and sought to connect his building to Observatorielunden, the surrounding park, and Sveavägen, with a space for a café and shops. Tengbom went even further in this respect in his nearby School of Economics. Here, larger spaces are stacked in an oval tower that looks out on Observatorielunden and an interior garden, since filled in with new construction.

FIGURE 1.7 Högalids Church, Ivar Tengbom, Stockholm, 1917–23

Source: C. G. Rosenberg photo, The Swedish Center for Architecture and Design, ARKM.1984-102-2293

Another common trait of some Neoclassical buildings in Stockholm of the twentieth century is an interest in evoking *the outside* on *the inside*. Tengbom's Concert Hall (1920–26) has an arched ceiling that he called "a glowing southern sky" and a painted portico as a backdrop to "lead a tired wanderer" (Knight 1982, 43). Tengbom, in fact, had in mind the memory of a visit to the Greek theatre at Segesta. This theatre, he wrote, "has such beauty and purity that the memory of it never fades: the eye is directed along rows of seats projecting powerfully from the cliff, over smoothly finished bands of stone spreading in waves; the intense sunlight fades into the landscape bounded by the blue horizon of the sea" (25) (Figure 1.9). Asplund's Skandia Cinema, located nearby, was also intended to suggest "festivity under a night sky." Elias Cornell suggests that this design was inspired by an evening festival that Asplund experienced in Taormina during his Grand Tour in 1914 (1986, 27).[11] In both cases, according to Knight, the architects are referring back to the lightness of garden architecture during the reign of Gustav III, when Desprez and Piper designed structures for Haga Park (Eriksson 1998, 68–69).[12]

These characteristics of Swedish Neoclassicism also reveal the influence of a diverse movement that carried several labels, including Neohumanism, Vitalism, and *Lebensphilosophie*. The impetus for the movement in Germany was philology, or the study of classics, dating from the time of Goethe and Hölderlin. The ultimate champion, however, was Friedrich Nietzsche, who was initially a philologist at the University of Basel. It was here where he wrote *The Birth of Tragedy*, a work that attempts to reconstruct the elements of pre-Homeric culture represented in early Greek drama. More specifically, he identified elements in the plays that were Apollonian (cerebral and dreamlike) and Dionysian (rhythmic, instinctive, and corporeal) (Nietzsche 2000, 17–62). The chorus, in particular, represented Dionysian themes which were inherent in the tragic narrative. Though his analysis was partly intended to advance classical scholarship, Nietzsche's larger motive was to use it as a tool of contemporary commentary. He wished in particular to denounce Socratic thinking (i.e., scientific thought) as a dead end and to promote "tragic knowledge, which in order to be tolerated, needs art as protection and remedy" (84). In Germany, his legacy was carried on by Stefan George, a prominent German poet, and his circle at the turn of the century, who advocated *Lebensphilosophie* or "philosophy of life." Later the tradition was sustained by Werner Jaeger through his writings about Greek ideals.[13]

German thinkers were particularly influential among Swedish writers in the early twentieth century. One source of Nietzschean influence arrived through the works of the Swedish poet Vilhelm Ekelund (1880–1949). In his book *Antikt Ideal* he describes the poetic qualities and literary history of some Mediterranean and continental landscapes while frequently digressing to mention the qualities of Skåne, his home province, and its poets (Ekelund 1909). The implication is that familiar Swedish landscapes have the capacity to be equally evocative and the consciousness of ancient places and writers can expand ways of thinking about them and fellow Swedes. The Greeks, "who had given the best expressions, the

FIGURE 1.8 View of Konserthus, Ivar Tengbom, Stockholm, 1920–26

Source: The Swedish Center for Architecture and Design, ARKM.1984-102-1747

FIGURE 1.9 View of interior of Konserthus, Ivar Tengbom, Stockholm, 1920–26

Source: The Swedish Center for Architecture and Design, ARKM.1984-102-1789

best, most informative formulations and rules of what is on the mind of man, are worth emulating" (Johannesson 1984, 218). For Ekelund, as for Nietzsche, the real value of an individual depends on his ability "to give quotidian experience the stamp of the eternal" (222). Life, in other words, is the practice of aesthetics. "The real task in life is to relate to the world in the manner of an artist" (218). Instead of morals, aesthetics points the way to "liberating states of mind, to joy and productivity" (218). In common with Nietzsche, he found that the best way to express these insights was through the art of the aphorism, the precise statement that can capture the substance of an entire book (225–28).

An even more significant conduit of Nietzschean thought in Sweden was August Strindberg, who had a short correspondence with the philosopher and dedicated several plays and novels to explaining his version of Nietzschean principles. One example is his novel *By the Open Sea*, about a well-educated government official who attempts to bring reform to an island community in the Stockholm archipelago. As in many works by Strindberg, he wishes to illuminate the double-sided quality of Nature, both benevolent and destructive. The protagonist alternates between a poetic and a scientific view of the surrounding landscape and struggles to control his erotic urges. His efforts to bring order to the community have tragic consequences, and he departs by sea at the end, reading the stars with different cultural meanings. He begins by thinking of the star of Bethlehem, which he quickly dismisses, and choses to see it as the star Beta in the constellation Hercules. "Away, towards the new Christmas star, across the sea, the All-mother, in whose lap was kindled the first spark of life; the inexhaustible bourne of fertility and life, the origin of life and its foe" (Strindberg 1913, 324).

This final passage from *By the Open Sea* suggests a diverse movement called Vitalism that stems both from Nietzsche's interest in the culture of pre-Homeric Greece and the thinking of Henri Bergson, articulated in his book *Creative Evolution*. The influence of Vitalism appears in sculpture and art throughout Scandinavia in the late nineteenth and early twentieth centuries, where nude figures are portrayed in Hellenic poses or simply at home in the natural world (Oelsner 2011). An artist's community in Denmark was committed to dressing in togas and living a rustic life like ancient Greeks, while others formed groups of like-minded naturists (163). Followers and opponents of Bergson, on the other hand, engaged in scientific discourse about the *élan vital* and whether a vital spark animates mechanism or whether it dwells within mechanism. Ernst Haeckel, author of the *Riddle of the Universe*, was a leader of Monism, a movement related to Vitalism. His great cause, shared by Strindberg in his spare time, was to prove the commonality of organic and inorganic matter, implying that the capacity or presence of life dwells within everything (Haeckel 1900).

Although the imprint of Strindberg's thinking and Vitalism can be seen in the multiple layers of meaning in Asplund's landscapes, it is less discernible in the development of landscape architecture in the early twentieth century in Sweden. Although this tradition is called Functionalist, it has a very different line of descent from its namesake in architecture. The programming of the aforementioned "nature" parks in Göteborg and Jönköping provide an example of how social programs, including temperance, recreation, and antiquarianism, were allied with the fundamental intention to preserve and enhance the existing qualities of the landscape. It was only later, in the second decade of the twentieth century, that Rutger Sernander (1866–1944), a professor of biology at Uppsala, campaigned to make these earlier innovations into a widely accepted doctrine for urban parks. He was critical of the design for St. Erik's park in Stockholm (1918) because it erased existing natural features of the site. "Sernander promoted the creation of a stylized landscape of pasture and grove that integrated the features of the local landscape with plant material sympathetic to the existing characteristics of the site" (Andersson 1993, 118). Stadsskogen (1916), a new park on the edge of Uppsala, became the exemplar of his approach (Figure 1.10). It was not until the thirties, however, that this kind of park was actively promoted by leaders in landscape design. Erik Lundberg, a professor of garden art at the Royal Institute of Technology, explained the two fundamental points of the new doctrine. One was to respond to existing conditions and "to enhance these aspects through emphasis and simplification, to augment the allure of natural beauty by picking and choosing" (118). The other was to attend to the responsibilities of the program by imagining "what comforts, recreation, and pleasures" would be possible at a particular site (118). National Romanticism was, in effect, sustained, though with more matter-of-fact methods.

This strategy assumed a more comprehensive guise in the hands of landscape architects at the Stockholm Department of Parks. These were the founders of the Stockholm School, which included Oswald Almqvist, director of the department

FIGURE 1.10 View of Stadsskogen, Uppsala, 1916

Source: Uppsala-Bild photo, County Museum of Uppland/Upplandsmuseet, UB019846

from 1936 to 1938, his successor, Holger Blom, and Erik Glemme, the landscape architect responsible for the most exemplary new parks in Stockholm. Though Blom was not a Social Democratic activist, he cultivated politicians to realize very large projects in the city. Besides hiring skilled people, his other gift was to clearly articulate the purposes of city parks:

> The park breaks up the unrelenting flow of urban construction. Taken as a group, parks can form a network in the urban fabric that provides citizens with necessary light and air. They can create borders between different parts of the city and provide each district with an individual character and identity.
>
> The park offers to citizens of all ages space for recreation, for promenades and for rest, for sports and play.
>
> The park is a place in which to gather: for concerts, demonstrations, parties, dance, and even religious services.
>
> The park preserves both nature and culture: existing nature and newly created; old traces of culture as well as modern additions.
>
> (Andersson 1993, 121)

One of the most significant achievements of the Stockholm School was Norr Mälarstrand, a sequence of parkland along the edge of Lake Mälaren that linked Fredhäll at the edge of the city to the Town Hall in the center (Figure 1.11). This included narrow portions that are manufactured nature along the edge of the lake, as well as Rålambshovsparken, a bowl-like clearing with a large outdoor performance space (Andersson 1993, 122–27). Another famous work was the restoration of Vasaparken in a dense residential neighborhood, when Torsgatan, a new street, was cut through existing rock on the site. Glemme used square rock gardens, defined by battered stone walls, to contrast with the random quality of the rocky site that remained (129–32). Finally, Tegnér Grove, a small hilltop park in the middle of the city, was also restored by Glemme (Figure 1.12). Here, the number of pathways was reduced to give prominence to the existing qualities of the landscape. Also, a pavilion was created on the the top of the hill that serves as a source for a meandering stream that flows into two ponds at the bottom of the hill. This sequence has continued to be a favorite place for children to bathe and play (128–29).

With the exception of works by Asplund, this pairing of National Romantic care for the natural world and concern for program did not have a counterpart in early Functionalist architecture, a movement that was preoccupied largely with efficient space, solar exposure, and means of construction. This new architectural agenda was inspired by work in Germany and France in the modern style, though it was labeled as "Functionalism" to emphasize a social agenda. Among left-leaning architects and intellectuals, it was felt that there was a new urgency to accommodate new programs associated with the welfare state. These would include schools, sports facilities, hospitals, transportation infrastructure, and, above all, housing. As Eva Rudberg notes, this new agenda included simplicity in construction, clarity in

FIGURE 1.11 View of Norr Mälarstrand, Erik Glemme, Stockholm, 1941–43

Source: C. G. Rosenberg photo, The Swedish Center for Architecture and Design, ARKM. 1962-101-0791

FIGURE 1.12 View of Tegnér Grove, Erik Glemme, Stockholm, 1941

Source: C. G. Rosenberg photo, The Swedish Center for Architecture and Design, ARKM. 1962-101-0799

forms, primacy of southern exposure, flat expression for facades, and the use of the high-rise to liberate the ground plane for parks (Rudberg 1998b).

The first examples of Functionalist architecture were built by KF (Kooperativa Förbundet), the engine of the cooperative movement in Sweden. Using their own architectural office, under the direction of Eskil Sundahl, they began by building factories and housing projects in the late twenties. Among them was the Luma light-bulb factory in Stockholm (Figure 1.13) and cooperative housing built for employees of the Three Crowns Flour Mill, near Stockholm (Childs 1947). The formal introduction of Functionalism, however, was the Stockholm Exhibition of 1930, designed by Asplund and others. His brilliant move was to promote Functionalist architecture and landscape as one indivisible package. Unlike the straightforward agenda of his Functionalist colleagues, however, he attempted to invoke historic memory into his designs that relate to the tent structures of Gustav III, the forum in Pompeii, and the maypole used on Midsummer's Eve, though it was lost on many at the time. To make his conception of the union of architecture and landscape unmistakable, he even built a restaurant with a grove of trees inside it. Though he used modern materials, Asplund's version of Functionalism had none of the exclusionary, uncompromising characteristics of many Functionalist projects, executed by more dogmatic Swedish architects that followed in the wake of the exhibition.[14] Instead, he gave landscape the preeminent role as the primary reference point for the architectural experience. It was not until the late thirties and early forties that his colleagues, after assessing the shortcomings of particular projects, began to rediscover the social potential of outdoor spaces and the importance of landscape (Rudberg 1998a, 119).

FIGURE 1.13 Luma Light Bulb Factory, Artur von Schmalensee, Stockholm, 1930

Source: Sune Sundahl photo, The Swedish Center for Architecture and Design, ARKM.1962-101-0592

Despite the initial shortcomings of Functionalism in Sweden, its advocates were acutely aware that their movement needed to follow the template set by National Romanticism by explaining broader cultural relationships.[15] Just as National Romantic painters sought to portray fundamental Swedish qualities in landscapes, apologists of Functionalism found that they needed to explain why their new thinking was also an authentic cultural product. In a polemical text called *acceptera* (1931), they attempted to make the case that Functionalism was not a rupture in time. Instead, following Geijer's dictum, they argued that it was deeply Swedish and was, in fact, passing on a tradition (Åhrén et al. 2008).

While this argument was not universally convincing at the time, it is true that boundaries between movements were not exactly hard and fast.[16] Classical scholars, inspired by the example of Ancient Greece, shaped National Romanticism. Twentieth-century Neoclassicism was in many respects an extension of National Romanticism, as it sought a reflection of a national identity in ancient buildings and landscapes. There was also a harbinger of Functionalism in the early "nature" parks, which were deeply influenced by National Romanticism. Because different agendas could coexist under the same movement, outside influences, though they were opposed by many at the time, were not necessarily an obstacle to realizing national ambitions or defining a national identity. The English Picturesque movement, for example, did provide a starting point towards a uniquely Swedish approach to landscape architecture. In the early twentieth century, in response to the loss of Norway in 1905, the Swedish national goals shifted to be *both* conscious of heritage, in the National Romantic spirit, and modern. Hjalmar Branting, a socialist politician, reassured Swedes in 1907 that, in spite of the revolutionary ideals of the socialists, they still intended to ensure that everyone could enjoy their cultural heritage (Barton 2005, 263). In this context, Neoclassicism was a model for Functionalism; it showed that Swedish architects could find a national expression within an international architecture.

This ambiguous milieu in the early part of the century that mixed progressive ambition and nostalgic longing was ideally suited for Asplund's gifts and inclinations. With the benefit of Nietzschean and Strindbergian thinking, it allowed a pathway to expand the appropriate, though predictable, thinking of the National Romantics toward an expression where classical, Norse, and progressive elements could coexist. In *Wir Philologen*, Nietzsche wrote, "a very precise retrospective analysis will lead us to the realization that we are the multiplication of many pasts" (Emden 2004, 387). Asplund recognized that the expression of this thinking ideally required landscape to achieve its aims; it was also the symbolic "forum" that everyone could understand within which he could create dialogues across time. He also recognized that this approach would not lend itself to any one fixed interpretation; by virtue of his poetic devices, he could allow the individual to take pleasure in reading a site as she or he might wish. While landscape had been, and continued to be, a source of Swedish identity and a vessel of progressive ideals, it also became an ambiguous domain for personal introspection.

Notes

1 See Magnus Olausson, "Fredrik Magnus Piper: The Man and His Work," in *Beskifning öfer Ideen och General-Plan till en Ängelsk Lustpark* (Stockholm, Sweden: Byggförlaget, 2004). Olausson awards the larger share of the credit for the picturesque gardens at Haga and Drottingholm to Gustav III.

2 Hagaparken is located near Solna in the northern suburbs of Stockholm.

3 *Frithjof's Saga* has been translated into many languages. The spelling of the hero's name can vary.

4 See Nolin 2013. Also see Catharina Nolin, *Till stadsbornas nytta och förlustande—den offentliga parken I Sverige under 1800-talet* (Stockholm, Sweden: Byggförlaget, 1999). One of the most important essays at this time was Nils Uno Blomberg's "Om naturparker" (1871). Rather than the beds of wildflowers favored by William Robinson, he advocated an approach where gardens or parks would be shaped from existing natural features, particularly existing groves of trees.

5 Images of famous paintings were frequently reproduced in *Läsebok for Folkskolan*, the national reader for schoolchildren, which was first published in the 1860s and continued into the twentieth century. While it also published essays on history and the natural sciences, it was a significant medium for inculcating national spirit. See Nolin 2013, 123.

6 See Lars Israel Wahlman, *Engelbrektskyrkan I ord och bild* (Stockholm, Sweden: Ernst Wessmans Bokförlag, 1925).

7 Early in his career Asplund was a close neighbor of Wahlman's and later married his wife. Wahlman was also part of the jury that selected the winner of the Woodland Cemetery Competition and later served on an advisory panel for the Cemetery. This family background is explained in Christina Engfors, ed., *E. G. Asplund: Architect, Friend, and Colleague* (Stockholm, Sweden: Arikitektur Förlag, 1990).

8 See *Den mindre trädgården. En bok för töppan och torpet* (1902), *Villaträdgården. En bok för sommarställen och stadsgårdar* (1903), *Herrgårdsträdgården* (1915).

9 Kenneth Frampton notes the importance of articles by Vilhelm Wanscher, a Danish architect and academic, published as early as 1907. See Kenneth Frampton, *Modern Architecture: A Critical History* (New York: Oxford University Press, 1980), 194.

10 See Simo Paavilainen, ed., *Nordic Classicism* (Helsinki, Finland: Museum of Finnish Architecture, 1982).

11 Cornell 1986, 27. Asplund wrote in his diary, "It was the last day of the carneval there and in the evening, there were coloured lanterns and funny coloured people and a big band on the square beneath the starry sky up there and with the roar of the sea deep down below."

12 In a review of the competition for the concert hall, Asplund wrote a glowing review of Tengbom's design. "The architecture is light and dissolved, the ceiling hovers unconfined, an effect of a tent à la Gustaviana on light tent poles. The light attractive space and the perspective towards the orchestra podium draw attention from the architecture into a boundless incorporeal space." This passage is quoted by Eva Eriksson (1998, 69).

13 See Werner Jaeger, *Paideia: The Ideals of Greek Culture* (New York: Oxford University Press, 1945).

14 Uno Ahrén's planning for Övre Johanneberg in the thirties in Göteborg comes to mind in this context. The Hjorthagen apartments by Hakon Ahlberg and Lief Reinius are another example of this tendency. Both give priority to solar orientation over hierarchies in public space. See Rudberg 1998a, 95–98.

15 Barbara Miller Lane treats this subject thoroughly in *National Romanticism and Modern Architecture in Germany and the Scandinavian Countries* (Cambridge: Cambridge University Press, 2000). She writes, in particular, of the difference in the reputation of National Romanticism after World War I in Germany and Sweden.

16 There was considerable resistance to Functionalism expressed by comments in the press both before and after the Stockholm Exhibition. Carl Malmsten, a furniture designer, was a leader among those who opposed it.

References

Åhrén, Uno, Gunnar Asplund, Wolter Gahn, Sven Markelius, Gregor Paulsson, and Eskil Sundahl. 2008. "Acceptera." In *Modern Swedish Design: Three Founding Texts*, edited by Lucy Creagh, Helena Kåberg, Barbara Miller Lane. New York: Museum of Modern Art.

Andersson, Thorbjörn. 1993. "Erik Glemme and the Stockholm Park System." In *Modern Landscape Architecture: A Critical Review*, edited by Marc Treib, 114–33. Cambridge, MA: MIT Press.

Barton, H. Arnold. 2005. "From Warfare to Welfare State: Sweden's Search for a New Identity." *Scandinavian Studies* 77 (3): 315–26.

Chambers, William. 1773. *A Dissertation on Oriental Gardening*. Dublin, Ireland: W. Wilson.

Childs, Marquis. 1947. *Sweden: The Middle Way*. New Haven, CT: Yale University Press.

Cornell, Elias. 1986. "The Sky as a Vault." In *Asplund*, edited by Claes Caldenby and Olof Hultin, 23–33. New York: Rizzoli.

Ekelund, Vilhelm. 1909. *Antikt Ideal*. Malmö, Sweden: Aktiebolaget Framtiden.

Emden, Christian. 2004. "The Invention of Antiquity: Nietzsche on Classicism, Classicality, and the Classical Tradition." In *Nietzsche and Antiquity*, edited by Paul Bishop, 372–90. Rochester, NY: Camden House.

Eriksson, Eva. 1998. "Rationalism and Classicism, 1915–30." In *Sweden: Twentieth Century Architecture*, edited by Claes Caldenby, Jöran Lindvall, and Wilfried Wang, 81–109. Munich, Germany: Prestel.

Facos, Michelle. 1998. *Nationalism and The Nordic Imagination*. Berkeley, CA: University of California Press.

Geijer, Erik. 1845. *History of the Swedes*. London: Whittaker and Co.

Haeckel, Ernst. 1900. *The Riddle of the Universe at the Close of the Nineteenth Century*. New York: Harper and Bros.

Hunt, John Dixon, and Peter Willis. 1993. *The Genius of Place: The English Landscape Garden, 1620–1820*. Cambridge, MA: MIT Press.

Johannesson, Eric. 1984. "Vilhelm Ekelund: Modernism and the Aesthetics of the Aphorism." *Scandinavian Studies* 56 (3): 213–34.

Karling, Sten. 1981. "From Tessin to Piper: A Century of Swedish Landscape Gardening." In *Fredrick Magnus Piper and the Landscape Garden*, edited by Karin Lindegren, 8–38. Stockholm, Sweden: Royal Academy of Fine Arts.

Knight, Stuart. 1982. "Swedish Modern Classicism in Context." *International Architect* 1 (8): 9–14.

Nietzsche, Friedrich. 2000. *The Birth of Tragedy*. Oxford: Oxford University Press.

Nolin, Bertil. 1996. "The Romantic Period." In *A History of Swedish Literature*, edited by Lars G. Warme, 150–203. Lincoln, NE: University of Nebraska Press.

Nolin, Catharina. 2004. "Public Parks in Gothenburg and Jönköping: Secluded Idylls for Swedish Townfolk." *Garden History* 32 (2): 197–212.

——. 2008. *En svensk lustgådskonst Lars Israel Wahlman som trädgårdsarkitekt*. Stockholm, Sweden: Bokförlaget Signum.

——. 2013. "Urban Parks in Sweden at the Turn of the Twentieth Century." In *Public Nature: Scenery, History and Park Design*, edited by Ethan Carr, Shaun Eyring, and Richard Wilson, 115–24. Charlottesville, VA: University of Virginia Press.

Oelsner, Gertrud. 2011. "Healthy Nature in Vitalism." In *The Spirit of Vitalism: Health, Beauty and Strength in Danish Art, 1890–1940*, edited by Gertrud Hvidberg-Hansen and Gertrud Oelsner, 158–97. Copenhagen, Denmark: Museum Tusculanum Press.

Olausson, Magnus. 1997. "National or International Style? From Nicodemus Tessin the younger to Fredrik Magnus Piper." *The Journal of Garden History* 17 (4): 267–77.

Rudberg, Eva. 1998a. "Building the Welfare of the Folkhemmet." In *Sweden: Twentieth Century Architecture*, edited by Claes Caldenby, Jöran Lindvall, and Wilfried Wang, 110–41. Munich, Germany: Prestel.

——. 1998b. "Early Functionalism, 1930–40." In *Sweden: Twentieth Century Architecture*, edited by Claes Caldenby, Jöran Lindvall, and Wilfried Wang, 81–109. Munich, Germany: Prestel.

Ståhl, Margareta. 2005. *Möten och Människor: Folkets Hus och Folkets Park*. Stockholm, Sweden: Bokförlaget Atlas.

Strindberg, August. 1913. *By the Open Sea*. Translated by Ellie Schleussner. New York: B. W. Huebsch.

2

THE WOODLAND CEMETERY PART I

Home, landscape, and death

Many scholars have classified displays of death as summations of distinctive worldviews. These have been designed to deliver messages of comfort and discomfort while also strengthening solidarity and excluding outsiders. Some nineteenth-century American cemeteries, such as Mount Auburn in Cambridge and Grove Street in New Haven, have sought to portray landscapes of desire, in the tradition of the English Picturesque movement. Another distinctive tradition, reflected in large public monuments in Washington, DC, attempts to confront death with the memory of a heroic life (Morris 2006, 204–24). Amidst these traditions, Stockholm's Woodland Cemetery presents a singular case study. Unlike a cemetery such as Mount Auburn, the Woodland Cemetery is not a portrait of one time and one worldview. Instead, as a result of construction over several decades, it reveals a transitional view of a changing country, struggling with modernity and memory. In this process, it shows intent to be inclusive by artful consolidation of pre-Christian, Christian, and Vitalist themes. In particular, it reveals an evolving conception of modernism and its capacity to embrace these themes. Finally, it shows how landscape is used with architecture to reach this end.

The changing ethos that underlies this creation was partly a product of a history largely unscathed by famine, war, or revolution in the past two centuries. This was due in large part to a consensus based on industry, neutrality, and a rejection of class conflict. Simultaneously drawing on the culture of the peasant and modern industrial values, Swedes used this consensus to develop an uncommon form of nationalism in the late nineteenth and early twentieth centuries. They did this with a moral imperative that rarely isolated problems; aesthetics, health, landscape, housing, and economic development were invariably thought of as one national cause. This new way of thinking, according to Arne Ruth, "retained significant elements of the tradition it was superceding. Swedish national culture would once more serve as a liberating force in the world. Sweden would build a new spiritual empire as the native land of modern values" (Ruth 1984, 85). This new mission, however, had an inherent contradiction with deep-seated values. Because the national ambition to be modern meant rapid urbanization, there was a massive displacement of the rural population in the early twentieth century and widespread anxiety about the disappearance of rural culture and landscape.

Collective memory under these circumstances was not a matter of national storytelling about tragedies and heroic victories. Instead, beginning in the nineteenth century, Swedes began to find a new ethos in the everyday: caring for the family in a beautiful and efficient home and appreciating a unique landscape. Just as home and landscape were united in life, the displays of death likewise offered the opportunity to comfort the bereaved by reminding them of the binding ties between family, culture, and landscape. The more difficult challenge was to claim that modern values—clarity, efficiency, and socialism—were not incompatible with an appreciation of family, culture, and landscape. The architects of the Woodland Cemetery, Gunnar Asplund and Sigurd Lewerentz, responded to this challenge and proposed a resolution of this perceived conflict.

The Stockholm Cemetery Authority announced a competition for an addition to Sandsborg Cemetery in 1914. This competition was won by Lewerentz and Asplund in 1915, thanks to their intention to preserve the existing forest and a subdued approach to monumentality (Figure 2.1). In contrast to the other competitors, many from Germany, Asplund and Lewerentz were very much in tune with this appreciation of native landscape, in the manner of those who designed "nature parks" in the nineteenth century.[1] The site was 120 acres in Enskede, a suburb to the south of the city's center (Figure 2.2). "The site, covered by a pine forest interspersed with spruce trees and various secondary growth, including birch, rowan, alder, and willow trees, was dotted with boulders and scarred by gravel pits, the remnants of a sand and gravel quarry" (Constant 1994, 29). In their winning competition entry, called "Tallum," they worked with the existing landscape, emphasizing the melancholy of graves in the dark forest and terracing the contours of the former gravel pits. Pathways, cut through the pine forest with names like the "Way of the Cross" and the "Way of the Seven Wells," allow processions of smaller ritualized sites (32). This return to the dark forest, a setting for many Swedish folktales, was an appeal to the collective memory of Old Sweden and served to make all graves equal in its dim light.

Swedish landscape, however, has more to offer than dark forests. First, the quality of light is distinctive. "In relation to misty Mediterranean horizons and the flat sky," writes Thorbjörn Andersson, "the northern bowl of heaven really is a bowl and on land its light is apparent even in its long mild shadows" (Andersson 1998, 230). Dawn and dusk are particularly long, with colors of "dull nuances of greys, greens and blues" (230). Because of the cold climate, there is a limited number of plant species, that, by virtue of the expression of artists and craftspeople, reinforces a widely shared affection for landscape. Finally, there is a consistent character to the landscape due to the glaciers ten thousand years ago, which caused a familiar pattern of concave and convex forms that varies little across Sweden (230).

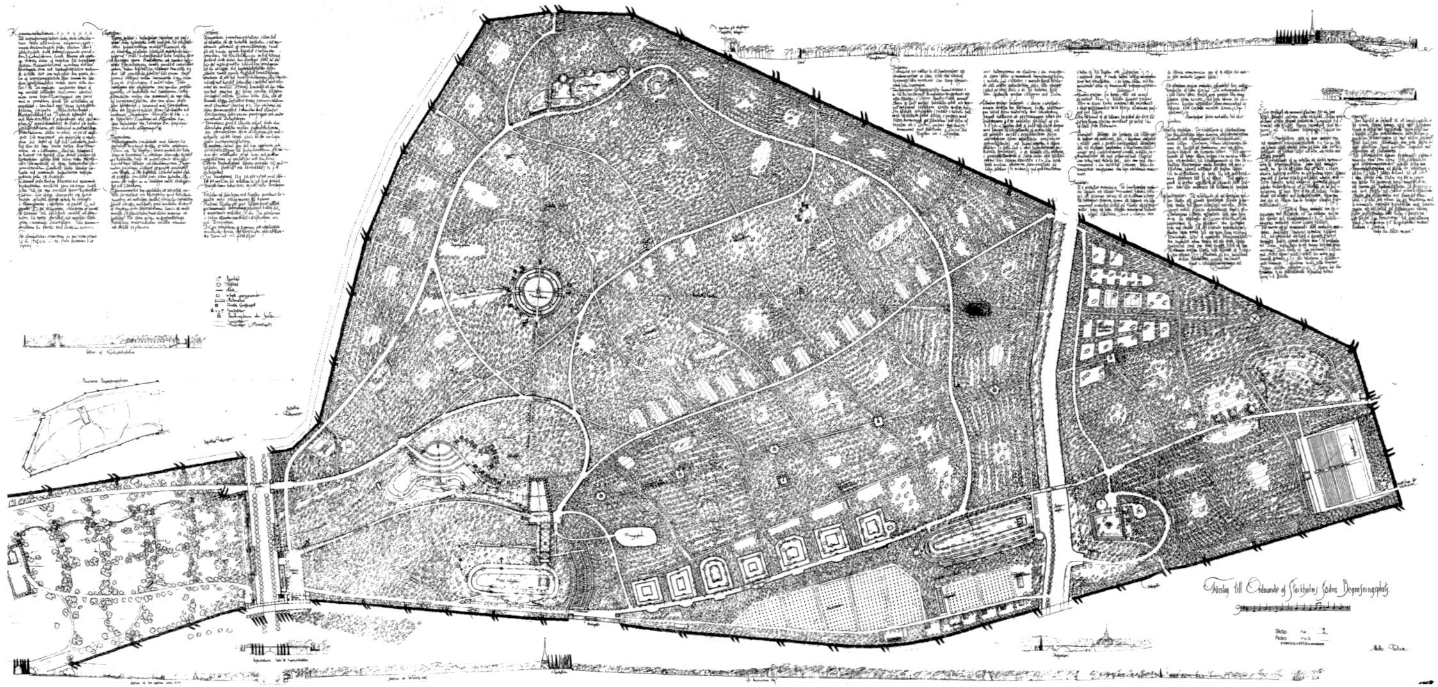

FIGURE 2.1 "Tallum" site plan, competition entry for the Woodland Cemetery, Asplund and Lewerentz, 1915

Source: Javier Beltran photo, The Stockholm Cemeteries Administration Archive

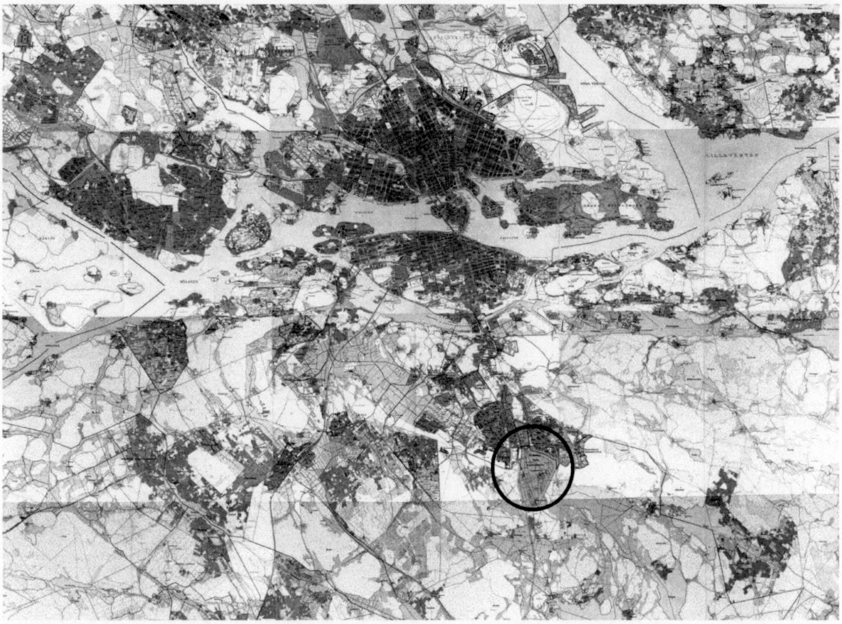

FIGURE 2.2 Map of Stockholm with location of Woodland Cemetery, 1934
Source: Map by H. Hellberg and A. E. Påhlman, Stockholm City Archive

Swedes have long enjoyed a comfort and identification with the essential character of this landscape. Andersson notes that unlike the culture of Middle Eastern countries, where gardens have become an expression of paradise very different from the arid landscape, Swedes have been content to find paradise in their existing environment (Andersson 1998, 230). Their sense of collective admiration of landscape is reflected in a code of shared rights of access called *allemansrätten*, a social code that governs access to private property. According to these rules, people have the right to traverse or overnight in a tent on the land of another. There is also the right to pick flowers and berries, but not nuts or twigs. With this background, "Swedes have an understanding that the natural world plays a decisive role in people's striving after both physical and also spiritual well being" (230). This feeling for Nature became a matter of nationalism in the late nineteenth century.

> Pine, fir and birch were seen as indigenous trees and so in a way represented Sweden, in paintings as well as *in situ*. According to long tradition, Swedish men and women believe they are fonder of Nature and the rural landscape than other peoples, that we have a certain feeling for Nature.
>
> (Nolin 2006, 125)

The Swedish version of Nature, which translated into care for forests and open spaces, was the emotional currency that everyone shared and became the setting for all significant memories, including childhood play, courtship, work, and family holidays.

This national pride, however, was not always expressed in what was built. For much of their preindustrial history, Swedish aristocrats followed the example of their larger European neighbors in the design of public buildings and landscapes. As mentioned earlier, Drottningholm Palace Garden was designed in the Baroque manner by Nicodemus Tessin the Younger in the late seventeenth century (see Figure 1.1). Haga Park in Stockholm was created by Frederic Magnus Piper and Gustav III in the style of the English Picturesque in the late eighteenth century (see Figures 1.3 and 1.4) (Andersson 1993, 117). The situation changed in the second half of the nineteenth century, when there was a search for a new national style in landscape. The municipal government of Stockholm seized the initiative during the late 1860s by beginning a policy to buy up large estates on the periphery of the city to preserve natural areas and limit speculation. At this time, there was widespread anxiety about urban growth and a will to preserve the memory of the wilder landscape. This movement was guided by the Lindhagen Plan of 1866, which established a principle that "no resident of the capital should be without a park in the vicinity, in other words that access to green areas was a right for the city's inhabitants" (Nolin 2006, 118). This forethought was providential because when city leaders took up the problem of scarce housing and cemetery space in the early twentieth century, they were in a strong position to intervene (Nilsson 2006, 102). They could shape a city that could respond to a growing industrial economy and allay the fears of a population uncomfortable with urbanism.[2]

Although these leaders were committed to a program to expand public parks in Stockholm in the early twentieth century, there was not yet a consensus on the design of the parks. In reaction to overly formal and derivative designs, Rutger Sernander, a professor of botany at Uppsala University, helped to form a new philosophy. He encouraged parks with "a stylized landscape of pastures and grove that integrated the features of the local landscape with plant materials sympathetic to the existing characteristics of the site" (Andersson 1993, 118). In his book *Stockholms Natur*, he praises the unique beauty of Swedish trees and cites different ways in which they have been integrated into urban environments. He shows examples of specific venerable trees in Stockholm that are treated like landmarks, something like memorials in Rome. He also draws attention to the unique beauty of rocky highlands and shorelines, characteristic of the geography of Stockholm (Sernander 1926). This appeal of rugged places can partly be explained by the rapid depopulation of rural areas. In 1850 more than 90% of the population lived in the country; by 1900, thanks to industrialization, this figure was reduced to 75%. Meanwhile, between 1845 and 1929, 1 million Swedes left for North America. With the departure of rural people, the typical Swedish landscape was slowly disappearing (Carlsson 1989, 21). Given the emotional significance of rural places for Swedes, this trend amounted to a growing crisis, both spiritual and demographic.

This anxiety about a changing country is captured in an artistic movement, previously mentioned, called National Romanticism, a collective search for national identity that began in the late nineteenth century. After a number of years of living in France, many Swedish artists began to see their country with fresh eyes and returned home in the 1880s eager to define a Nordic identity (Facos 1998). They found a country that, despite industrialization, still had a sense of itself. "The daily life of most people was closely allied to the conditions of Nature and the changing seasons. A feeling for Nature is also deeply rooted in Nordic tradition and has characterized myths and popular stories since time out of mind" (Eriksson 1998, 19). A group of artists called the Artists' Association, formed in 1886, began to paint subjects featuring northern evenings, pine forests, and rural people in everyday activities (19). The cultural dichotomy of the period was evident at the Stockholm Art and Industry Exhibit of 1897. On one hand, there were exhibits that expressed optimism about the future and technology. On the other, "it expressed an interest in Nature, backward looks, and care about tradition, where change could imply a threat to essential values" (20). This expresses the fundamental tension that Gunnar Asplund and Sigurd Lewerentz confronted later with the design of the Woodland Cemetery.

This tense union between tradition and modernism also happened in the development of the Swedish home. What began as an effort to sustain Swedish identity by preserving rural craft and architecture later inspired a movement that embraced beauty in the home as a force of social regeneration. This in turn had its impact on successive exhibitions and new progressive housing programs in the early twentieth century. Artur Hazelius, a linguist, began the movement by founding both the Nordic Museum (1873), dedicated to Nordic rural crafts, and Skansen (1891), a museum of rural architecture. At the same time, Carl Larsson gave this movement significance in the art world by moving his family to a farmhouse called Lilla Hyttnäs at Sundborn in Dalarna, a province that maintained its folk traditions. Over many years, he and his wife Karin transformed this house with colors, textile, and furniture in a style that is both vernacular and original. He made many paintings, presented in his book *Et Hem*, which document both the spaces and family life. His example showed how beautiful domestic environments can be stimulating places to raise children. It is noteworthy that the Larssons began the tradition of painting eighteenth-century Swedish chairs pearl white, a model for Asplund's chairs in the Woodland Chapel.

Larsson was fundamentally a conservative by instinct, but he inspired many thinkers who were decidedly progressive. Among the most important of them was Ellen Key, who became the advocate for this cult of the domestic. In a pamphlet called *Beauty for All* and a book called *Beauty in the Home*, she made a case for the close relationship between beauty and utility for furnishing and decorating the home. She wrote, "you work better, feel better, become friendlier and more joyful if you surround yourself in your home with beautiful shapes and colors" (Key 2008, 55). She also insisted that beauty in the home was not a luxury only reserved for the wealthy; with educated taste, all classes could enjoy its benefits. In particular, she observed that all things take on an enhanced beauty when you are able "to discern its true purpose" (38).

Gregor Paulsson, an art historian and theorist, took inspiration from Ellen Key, among others, and campaigned for a new approach to machine-made products for the home. As head of the Swedish Arts and Crafts Society, he organized the Home Exhibition of 1917 to introduce modern designs for the home. Because it addressed the extreme shortage of adequate homes for workers in urban areas, housing was the real motive for the show. Paulsson, like Key, wanted to demonstrate that the housing crisis was an aesthetic, social, and economic problem (Kåberg 2008, 65). He later went on to organize the Stockholm Exhibition of 1930, with the purpose of promoting design innovation in housing and furnishings.

In this context of reconceiving the modern Swedish home in the early twentieth century, other progressive groups were campaigning for a new conception of the urban cemetery. Swedes at the time had the benefit of new thinking in Europe about the design of cemeteries, cremation, and death. After much reluctance on the part of the Swedish Lutheran Church, cremation had gained acceptance as hygienic and pragmatic (Constant 1994, 15). In addition, Maurice Maeterlinck, a Belgian dramatist who wrote a book called *Death* in 1913, was particularly influential. He advocated a clearer conception of death, unencumbered by cultural mythology and instinct. "Here begins the open sea," he wrote, "here begins the wonderful adventure, the only one to be worthy of man's enquiring mind, the only one to raise itself as high as his highest yearning. May we become used to regarding death as a form of life, a form as yet we do not understand" (Johansson, 1996, 15). His book was widely read by advocates of cremation in Sweden and served for many as a foundation for a modern conception of death (Constant 1994, 17). Another important precedent for twentieth-century groups was the *Waldfriedhof* (1907), an influential cemetery designed by Hans Grässel, a municipal architect in Munich. It was sited in a forest and broken down into intimate units (14).

As in the *Waldfriedhof*, Lewerentz and Asplund preserved the poché of the existing pines across the whole site, while high points were marked with columbaria of different sizes and small clearings were made for groups of graves. Two existing through-roads were preserved, and other looping roads were made to define larger districts. The main architectural intervention was a vaulted chapel with a tall tower that was to be located somewhat close to the north entrance. Its façade was located off-center in relation to a keystone-shaped forecourt (Figure 2.3). The existing gravel pit at the north end, meanwhile, was preserved as a sunken garden. One of the main organizing ideas was the "Way of the Seven Wells," an axial route that extended across the site (see Figure 2.1). Asplund and Lewerentz also produced several vignettes, using plan, section, and elevation drawings. Among the most compelling of these were plans that explained how graves could be placed in the forest and a perspective of a leaning cross at the beginning of the "Way of the Cross" (Figure 2.4).

The consistently modest scale of the forest clearings and looping roads gives the plan the quality of a suburb. In fact, the jurors, despite their enthusiasm, advised the architects to make a larger clearing to relieve the monotony of the forest (Constant 1994, 44). One of the strengths of the scheme, however, was that the

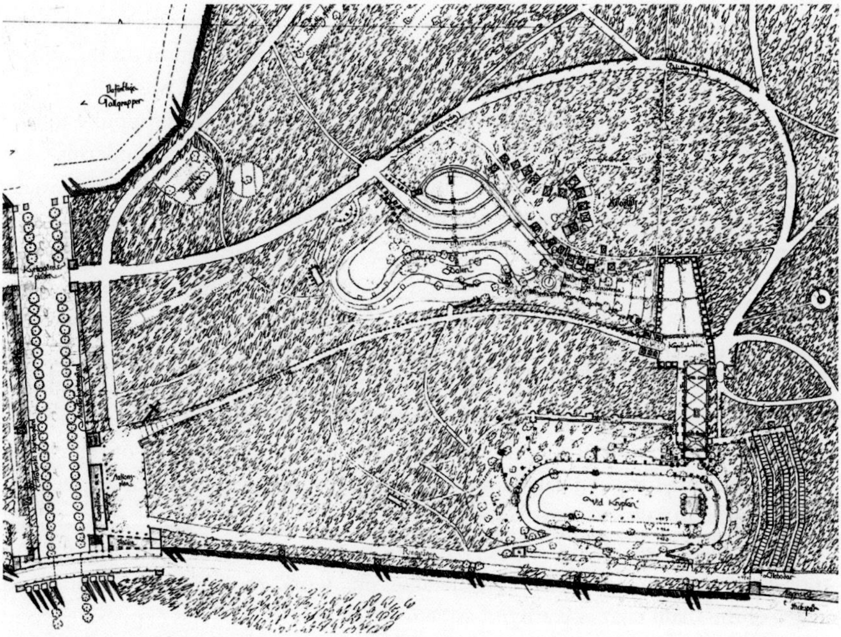

FIGURE 2.3 Detail of "Tallum" competition entry showing "Way of the Cross," chapel, and forecourt, Woodland Cemetery, Asplund and Lewerentz, 1915

Source: Javier Beltran photo, The Stockholm Cemeteries Administration Archive

FIGURE 2.4 Sketch vignettes from "Tallum" competition entry, Woodland Cemetery, Asplund and Lewerentz, 1915

Source: The Swedish Center for Architecture and Design, ARKM.1988-104-0921

episodic and non-monumental quality would lend itself to construction by phases over time. It also allowed rather dramatic revision, where improvisation on the part of the Cemetery Authority was mixed with periodic reconsideration on the part of the architects. During this process, which spanned decades, there was both a motivation to sustain the qualities of the scheme from 1915 as well as an impulse to find a monumental quality that was missing. Meanwhile, new ideas of modernity, including Neoclassicism and Functionalism, came to the forefront while the Social Democrats were gathering more support in the country.

One of the schemes that attempted to create greater clarity in the cemetery, if not a monumental spirit, was made by Lewerentz in 1918. Here he shows a large exedra at the north entrance, which was later built, and an axis that extends visually across an existing gravel pit to end at the rear of a chapel that is engaged in a narrow forum of columbaria that extends east to west (Figure 2.5). The chapel was to be the so-called Little Chapel designed by Asplund. In its schematic form it has a deeply recessed portico for gathering, an almost square form of the chapel with an aedicula between catafalque and altar. The space emphasized the vertical dimension with two vertical windows on the east and west walls that would provide daylighting.[3] The Cemetery Authority, however, lacked funding for this stone-built structure and the considerable site work required. The siting and design of the main chapel were put aside in 1918 in favor of a less expensive wood and stucco chapel to be designed by Asplund in the forest (Constant 1994, 55).

The outcome was the Woodland Chapel, which was swiftly conceived by Asplund in 1918 and completed by 1921. The chapel sits within a walled enclosure within the forest, reminiscent of a country churchyard, just southeast of the high point at the north end (Figure 2.6) (Constant 1994, 63). The scale is modest and domestic, inspired by a Danish eighteenth-century estate called Liselund, where buildings have a combination of vernacular and classical themes (Johansson 1996,

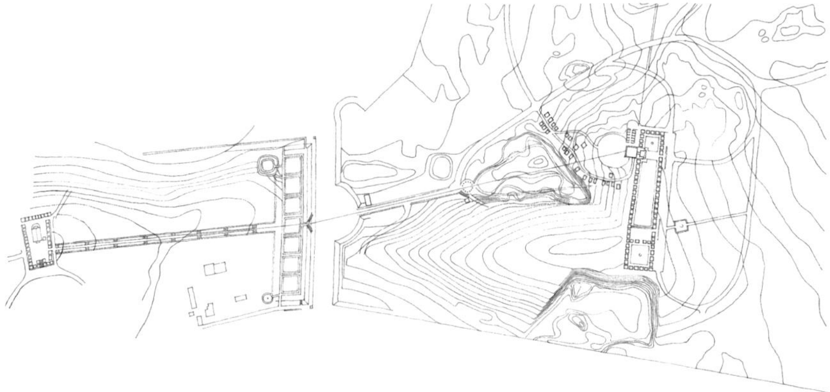

FIGURE 2.5 North Entry plan of 1918, Woodland Cemetery, Lewerentz

Source: Author drawing after Lewerentz

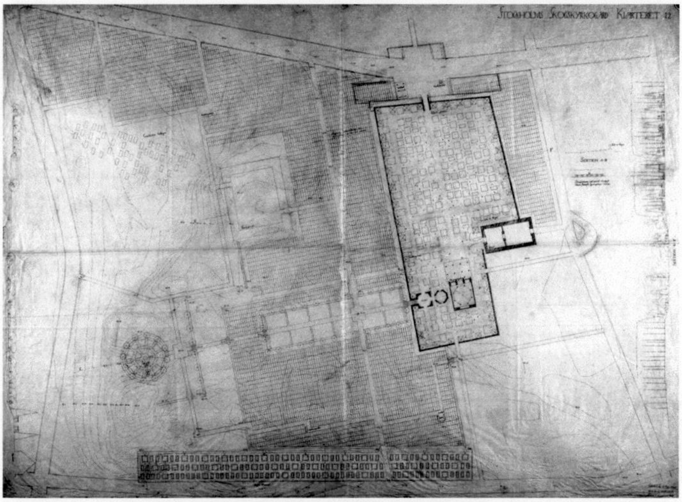

FIGURE 2.6 Site Plan, Woodland Chapel, Asplund, 1922–23

Source: The Swedish Center for Architecture and Design, ARKM.1988-02-3447

61). There is a deep low porch with rows of columns that relate to the columnar pines nearby. It also invites entry and serves as a preliminary gathering place (Figure 2.7). The interior is a startling contrast, evoking the Cosmos with a skylight plaster dome—a miniature Pantheon (Cornell 1986). This grand gesture is balanced by an intimate circle of chairs for the funeral party (Figure 2.8). The result is very effective at capturing the traditional Swedish themes of landscape and home, while also introducing prehistoric and classical motifs.

The sequence of entry begins with a very spare gabled structure that serves as a gateway. This is called a *stiglucka* in Swedish and is a typical feature of country churchyards (Figure 2.9). There is a small medallion above the gate featuring a small temple and an old tree that surrounds it.[4] The expression "hodie mihi, cras tibi" (today me, tomorrow you) is inscribed within the temple. The tunnel-like view through the gatehouse focuses on the front façade of the chapel, which can be seen in the distance. Within the enclosure there are no graves, unlike the typical churchyard. Instead the walled enclosure serves to frame a grove of towering pine trees, a pre-Christian version of a sacred place. Once a visitor is past the gateway, Asplund has already used three methods—literary, spatial, and cultural—to prepare the bereaved. First, there is the Latin saying to remind about one's own mortality. Second, the spatial transition of the confined tunnel indicates a significant change to a different place. Finally, the walled churchyard that encloses a forest uses a familiar cultural type to present an even older one.

The scale of the chapel seen straight ahead is modest in the context of the towering pine trees (Figure 2.10). From a distance, the roof is partly obscured by pine trees that were left to grow in the forecourt. In particular, Asplund shows a tree in his preliminary sketches to the left of the main axis (Figure 2.11). Though

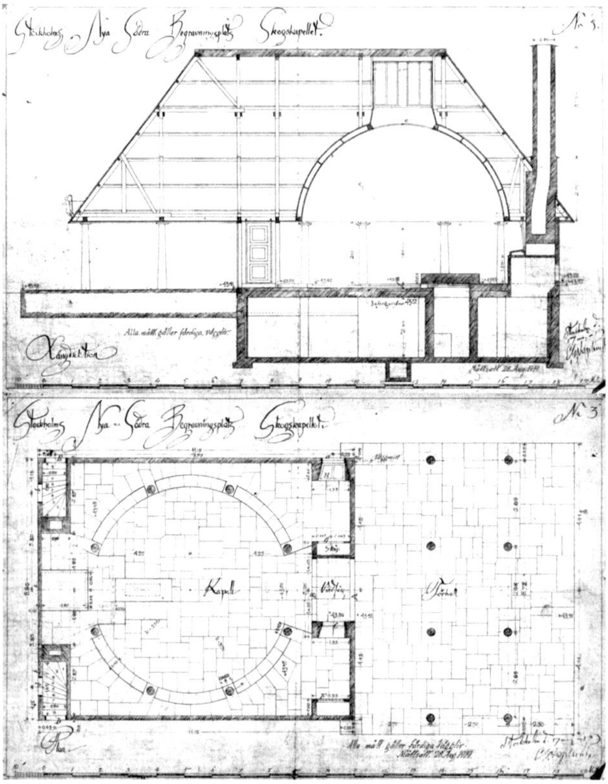

FIGURE 2.7 Woodland Chapel plan and section, Woodland Cemetery, Asplund, 1919

Source: The Swedish Center for Architecture and Design, ARKM.1988-02-3360, ARKM.1988-02-3359

FIGURE 2.8 Woodland Chapel interior view, Woodland Cemetery, Asplund, 1918–21

Source: C. G. Rosenberg photo, The Swedish Center for Architecture and Design, ARKM. 1988-104-0619

it may not be the same tree, there remains a tree in this position to this day. This decision can be seen to achieve a number of things. It defers to the order of the forest. At the same time, it acts as scaling device that contrasts the giant height of the tree and the diminutive size of the chapel. It also serves as a veil for the structure, thereby heightening interest, following a principle of the Picturesque.[5]

The forecourt of the chapel is a modest gravel area that organizes a partially submerged structure with an earth roof for the storage of coffins before services (Figure 2.12). On the south side this roof is broken by a small lunette window. In addition, next to this structure there is also an enigmatic fountain in the shape of a small gatehouse where the recessed area that would denote entry is painted black. As one stands before the chapel, before entering the portico, it is quite easy to inspect Carl Milles's *Angel of Death*, perched on the roof just above the entry on the main axis (Figure 2.13). This sculpture is shown in the 1919 schematic drawings of the chapel made by Asplund, although the sculpture was not finished until 1921.[6] The original sculpture was made of hammered copper, but has since been replaced by a composite copy that is painted gold. It shows a winged nude woman with a generous figure, her arms open. Soon after the chapel opened, the sculpture aroused some critical reaction among clergy, one of whom denounced it as "indecent and offensive." Asplund promptly responded with incredulity, claiming that this "angelic figure" with "a countenance of mild melancholy" welcomes "the dead and the miserable" as "a metaphor of the savior" (Constant 1994, 59).

The fundamental character of the design, however, was not controversial. As previously mentioned, Asplund was inspired by a late eighteenth-century Danish estate called Liselund by Andreas Kirkerup (1792–95) on the island of Møn, which he had recently visited (Jones 2006, 67). Constant adds that he was most attracted to the gardener's house, called *hytten* (or cottage), a rustic house that resembles a Viking dwelling, located at the base of a Bronze Age tumulus. One can guess that Asplund would have been interested in the way that trees were once planted at this cottage to correspond to column bays (Figure 2.14). The manor house, meanwhile, also represented an attractive blend of vernacular and classical motifs, with a thatched hipped roof and Doric columns. The rear wing, in particular, has a surrounding shallow porch with Doric columns. Just as the churchyard and grove are simultaneously vernacular and pre-Christian, Liselund is both vernacular, if not archaic, and classical.

Asplund's skill was to reduce the elements of this precedent to an extremely compact form that accommodates the program and allows telling details to be appreciated. One of his most effective adjustments from this model was the proportional relationship between roof and portico. He reduced the height of the columns to approximately seven feet, thereby increasing the presence of the simple hipped roof and making an inviting human scale. Also, at this height, the portico can be seen clearly under the branches of the pines. Meanwhile the depth of the portico invites you in and creates a generous gathering place for before and after services. There are twelve columns, three bays wide and two bays deep. The middle bay is slightly wider in deference to the axis of the entrance. The floor,

FIGURE 2.9 Woodland Chapel gateway, Woodland Cemetery, Asplund, 1919

Source: Holger Ellgaard photo

FIGURE 2.10
Distant view of Woodland Chapel, Woodland Cemetery, Asplund, 1918–21

Source: Author photo

FIGURE 2.11
Asplund sketch of Woodland Chapel, Stockholm, 1918

Source: Canadian Center for Architecture/ Centre Canadien d'Architecture, DR 1984:1644

FIGURE 2.12 Earthen structure, Asplund, Woodland Chapel, 1918–21

Source: Author photo

FIGURE 2.13 "*Angel of Death*," Carl Milles, Woodland Chapel, 1921

Source: Author photo

FIGURE 2.14 "Hytten" at Liselund, Andreas Kirkerup, Møns, Denmark, 1792–95

Source: L. Piggot photo, Wikimedia Commons

paved with stone, is at the same level as the surrounding grade, making an easy transition.

Other compelling details relate to the design of the columns. First, they have no base; the columns sit directly on the stone paving, a decision that makes them subject to rot and runs contrary to good practice (Figure 2.15). Like the wood siding that goes to the ground at his house at Stennäs from 1938, this was done with an aesthetic intention. The most obvious explanation is that they are meant to imitate the quality of a tree as it grows directly from the ground. This is seen even more forcefully later from the inside of the chapel, where one can look out to see flanking columns and corresponding pine trees beyond. The other aspect of the columns is the detailing at the capital. Above the wide but thin echinus is an abacus that is painted black (Figure 2.16). This is separated from the ceiling by a deep recessed joint. One impression is that the roof is meant to appear to be floating without bearing any load on the columns. Another impression suggests that the column is to be seen as a separate unit, both enhancing its association with the pine trees and drawing attention to its human scale.

Before entering the chapel, there is one more transition that is analogous to the gatehouse. It is a very small hallway with two sets of doors. The outside one is solid, with irregular plates of iron and a skull lock, also made from wrought iron. The inside door, again made of wrought iron, was made by Petter Andersson, a popular blacksmith among architects.[7] The door's design by Asplund is a filigree that obscures the view, akin to looking at the sky through the branches of pine trees (Figure 2.17). Asplund intended that only the inside door should be closed during a service so the bereaved could look out and, thanks to flanking columns, appreciate the connection of columns to pine trees even more forcefully.[8] Soon after the opening of the Chapel, a layer of glass was added to the door for thermal comfort.

The interior of the Chapel is a plastered dome with roof-lit oculus, surrounded by eight columns where the radius of the dome is approximately one foot below the height of the columns (see Figure 2.7). There is no entablature where the dome meets the columns, which sit on the edge of two steps. In this way, according to Elias Cornell, the illusion of the sky can extend right to the floor, the presumed horizon. Meanwhile, the plan of the dome is inscribed on the floor by virtue of the steps, which correspond to the circle above. There is a primary axis from the door that ends in a sunken arch that frames an altar (see Figure 2.8). White-painted Gustavian chairs are placed in two crescents on either side of the axis.[9] The catafalque for the coffin is placed on axis in front of the altar, between the seated rows. Asplund's early interior sketches show a painting before the altar, which was later created by Gunnar Torhamn and portrayed the risen Christ.[10]

The contrast between the domestic exterior and the cosmic interior involve several layers of memory. First, because the structure is very small, only those most intimate with the deceased can attend. As a result, the deceased is remembered as a member of a family, rather than a public figure. The circle places them in relationship to each other and the body, rather than an altar. This reflects the

FIGURE 2.15 Columns at Woodland Chapel, Asplund, 1918–21

Source: N. Åzelius photo, The Swedish Center for Architecture and Design, ARKM.1988-104-0616

FIGURE 2.16 Column capital, Asplund, Woodland Chapel, 1918–21

Source: Author photo

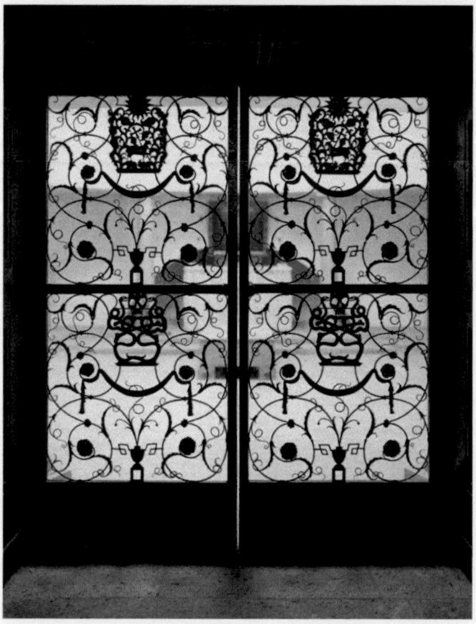

FIGURE 2.17 Iron door at Woodland Chapel, Asplund, 1918–21

Source: C. G. Rosenberg photo, The Swedish Center for Architecture and Design, ARKM.1988-104-0624

priorities popularized by Carl Larsson and Ellen Key, where the family and home were of preeminent importance. On another level, the domestic scale speaks to how the dead were remembered in homes in rural Sweden. The dome of the Pantheon, however, introduces a new dimension of memory. It comes as a surprise to see an illusion of the sky coming from the forest, where the view of it is concealed. This gesture defies conventions of Christian design dictating nave and sanctuary and returns the bereaved to a pre-Christian concept of space and the Cosmos. By doing this, it suggests that death can introduce an unexpected experience of time and space, a variation on Maeterlinck's idea of a journey to the unknown.

This pre-Christian sensibility suggests that while remembering the life of an individual, the bereaved should also be aware of a bond between body, earth, and sky. While the bereaved sit before the body, they have the dome of the sky above them and the view of the portico and forest to one side. Between the reality of mortality, an abstraction of the Cosmos, and the tangible beauty of the pine forest with all of its cultural resonance, they are in a position to make their own reading. One person might see how death is part of home, family, and landscape, but also connects all of these to a limitless realm, best represented by the sky. Another individual might see the coexistence of cerebral abstraction and sensuality in daily life. This particular intention to unite sky, body, and landscape characterizes a number of projects, including the Stadsbibliotek, the Skandia Cinema, and the Woodland Crematorium.

This link between body and Cosmos is also suggested by the previously mentioned sculpture, *Angel of Death* (1921) by Carl Milles (see Figure 2.13), perched on the roof of the Woodland Chapel. It functions as a quiet *memento mori*, but the message is not as explicit as those found in early American cemeteries. Though she has wings, this angel is nude in the mode of a Neolithic earth goddess, with generous breasts, belly, and hips. A figure of the heavens, in other words, has been portrayed as a symbol of earthly fertility. The wings, in fact, appear to have straps, as if they are not a natural part of her body. Like both building and landscape, the sculpture is a composite of two very different traditions. Some visitors might miss this ambiguity completely. Others might appreciate the gentle irony. Still others might know that the "Angel of Death" was an old woman who presided over the cremation of Viking chieftains. Finally, there are those who might see it as a promise of maternal care and rebirth beyond this life. In any case, it is not intended to inspire fear but to welcome all the bereaved, with their different hopes, fears, and expectations. Instead of shunning all symbolism, an effort has been made to artfully consolidate traditions for spiritual solidarity in the face of death.

The earthly side of the *Angel of Death* can be described as a variation on Vitalism, a diverse movement, mentioned in the introduction, that derives partly from the early thinking of Nietzsche, explained in *The Birth of Tragedy*. It also stems from a philosophical inquiry, dating from the time of Aristotle, that posed questions about whether life can be explained purely as a matter of mechanism or as a matter of a force animating that mechanism. In the early twentieth century, Henri Bergson's conception of the *élan vital* was the most noteworthy version of this branch of philosophy. Bergson explored, in particular, the finality of the parts and the whole of a given organism. If one traces any organism, or part, back to its origins, all are related to the same "protoplasmic jelly" (Bergson 1911, 43). "In this sense each individual may be said to remain united with the totality of living beings by invisible bonds" (43).

It was an easy step for artists and poets in Sweden to extend this idea to a bond between humanity and landscape. In the 1890s, many artists left the cities to join colonies in the country in order to be closer to the natural world. Among them were J. A. G. Acke and Eugene Jansson, who pioneered "Open-Air Vitalism" in painting between 1904 and 1910. Acke is notable for seascapes with nudes, where the viewer is invited to appreciate the analogy between forces of nature and the latent power of the human body. Though he never wrote about Vitalism and was a professed agnostic, Asplund reveals a deep interest in the presence of the human form in projects spanning decades. His Snellman House, from 1917, features a womb room, and the Lister County Courthouse has balusters with an unmistakable bulge (Wrede 1980, 57–64). In addition, his vacation house in Stennäs, discussed in Chapter 6, has a memorable swelling fireplace, positioned on a staircase. Though its presence is subdued in the early phases of the cemetery, Vitalism is the philosophical underpinning of the alternative spirituality expressed at the cemetery. Like Asplund's union of antiquity with Swedish vernacular at the Woodland Chapel, the *Angel of Death* demonstrates how Vitalist messages will be linked to other memorial forms in later phases of the cemetery.

These themes, however, were not sustained in the second phase of development of the cemetery (1923–30). For both landscaping and architecture, this phase was largely undertaken by Sigurd Lewerentz. The Resurrection Chapel, designed by Lewerentz in 1923, reveals a different approach that was inspired by his interest in Neoclassicism. It is located at the southern end of the cemetery and receives the axis of the "Way of the Seven Wells," taking a more public site than the Woodland Chapel (Figure 2.18). Lewerentz enhanced the long "Way of the Seven Wells" with taller spruce trees to emphasize the edge (Constant 1994, 105). Once one approaches the chapel there is a walled passage of close to one hundred feet that focuses the view on the front portico, analogous to the walled passage that would later define the North Entry. Immediately in front of the chapel there is a paved court that includes a waiting pavilion immediately to the east. To the west there is a sunken garden with graves, defined on one side by a building with a long colonnade which resembles an ancient Greek stoa.

Because of the requirement to orient the chapel on an east–west axis, a separate entry portico is used to receive the axis from the north. The independence of this portico is expressed by a slight skew that is barely perceptible on the site. Another curious detail is the deep reveal at the eave, which lends a floating quality to the

FIGURE 2.18 Resurrection Chapel exterior view, Lewerentz, 1923–26

Source: The Swedish Center for Architecture and Design, ARKM.1973-103-035)

thin roof structure. The lofty interior is illuminated by one large south-facing window that allows the visitor to barely make out the ghostly presence of pilasters that surround the room (Figure 2.19). Once a service is over, mourners leave from a small door on the west side, in the middle of the gable end. From here they are able to proceed down stairs to enter the sunken garden with random fir trees amid graves (Figure 2.20). This garden, in turn, is engaged axially with four large square areas, divided into quadrants that are devoted to gravesites as well. Due to the lack of trees, this was one of the first grave precincts to be developed in the cemetery (Constant 1994, 183). As an urban grid, constructed with earthworks, it is far closer in spirit to Lewerentz's Malmö Eastern Cemetery (1916–73) (Figure 2.21).

Lewerentz purposefully posed a very difficult problem for himself. The chapel, as he conceived it, needed to be a monument that would terminate the "Way of the Seven Wells" in addition to creating a convincing relationship with the neighboring cemetery quadrants. His dual purpose is reflected in the separation of the chapel into two parts that do not touch. Though he uses Neoclassicism brilliantly to create an otherworldly quality to the interior of the chapel and to receive the axis, it is not effectively associated with the surrounding landscape. Asplund's formula of sky, body, and earth is not repeated. Because the arrival sequence is formal along a long axis, there is no effective interplay between interior and exterior experience.

FIGURE 2.19
Resurrection Chapel interior view, Lewerentz, 1921–25

Source: The Swedish Center for Architecture and Design, ARKM.1973-103-084-044

FIGURE 2.20
Sunken Court, Resurrection Chapel, Lewerentz, 1921–25

Source: The Swedish Center for Architecture and Design, ARKM.1973-103-084-019

FIGURE 2.21
Resurrection Chapel aerial view, Lewerentz, 1921–25

Source: The Swedish Center for Architecture and Design, ARKM.1962-102-076

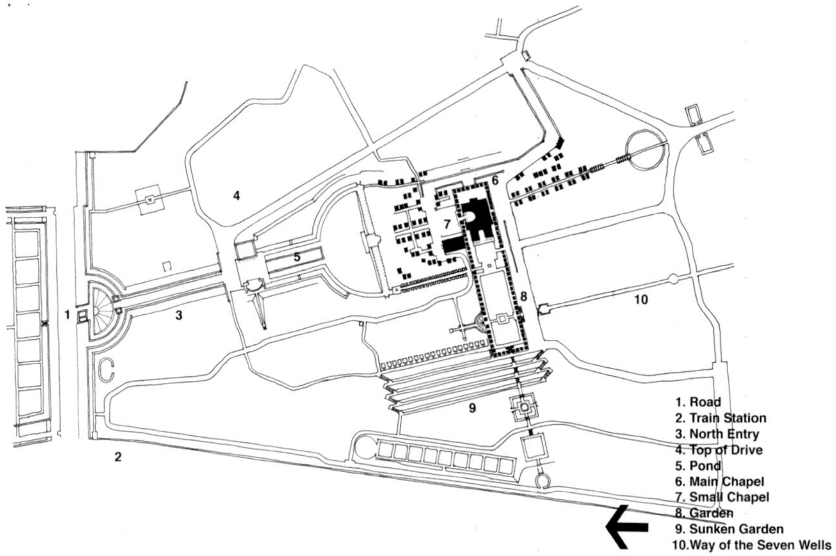

FIGURE 2.22 North Entry plan 1920 at Woodland Cemetery, Lewerentz

Source: Author drawing after Lewerentz

While it is possible to think of the chapel as a villa with its Italian garden of graves, neither chapel nor grave quadrants strengthen or complement the original conception of the cemetery. It is fair to add that Lewerentz had in mind a complete revision of the original conception as well. Briefly, before the Resurrection Chapel was designed, he conceived a vision of the North Entry in 1920 as an axial sequence leading to a Neoclassical precinct that also received a cross-axis from a more intimate garden to the west (Figure 2.22). Though it satisfied a need for monumentality and solved the formal problem of a shift in axis, it also asserted the preeminence of architecture over landscape. Perhaps anticipating swift rejection, Lewerentz never showed the design to the Cemetery Board (Constant 1994, 66).

In many respects, though it happened in an accidental way, the Woodland Chapel represented a more promising starting point for the future design of the crematorium and North Entry of the cemetery. Some of its innovations can be called "modern" in that they responded to an early twentieth-century Swedish anxiety about urban life and the loss of rural culture, the devotion to home, archetypal landscapes, and increasing diversity in religious belief. Chief among them is a concept where vernacular ideas are paired with pre-Christian ones to create statements of compelling ambiguity. The site plan is both churchyard and sacred grove; the sculpture is both angel and earth goddess; the chapel is both hut and "pantheon." In each of these cases, there is an implied resolution between qualities such as earth and sky, humble and extraordinary, wild and civilized, abstract and sensual that depend on each other for definition. This kind of resolution could be said to reduce antagonism between people or within an individual; beliefs and impulses that have been regarded as opposed can be seen to coexist. Also, thanks to the use of both vernacular and archaic elements, there is an impression of compressed time; the past, embedded in both landscape and architecture, becomes a vision of eternity that is not vacant and irrelevant but full of significance for the present.

Despite the differences in the qualities of the Woodland and Resurrection Chapels, it is important to remember that Tallum was the conceptual beginning of the careers of both Asplund and Lewerentz. It was neither a concrete nor a perfect vision. Although compelling in the cultural union of death and the forest, it posed the problems of the place of architecture in the landscape and the role of monumentality. As the competition jurors noted, it lacked a sense of sequence or release from the forest. It did, however, establish a principle about the primacy of landscape. During the Neoclassical period, Lewerentz, in particular, struggled with this principle and a desire for monumentality. In Asplund's case, the resolution of this dilemma became the theme of his career. The Stadsbibliotek presented itself as the next opportunity to create another solution.

Notes

1 See Catharina Nolin, "Public Parks in Gothenburg and Jönköping: Secluded Idylls for Swedish Townsfolk," *Garden History* 32, no. 2 (2004): 197–212. Also see Catharina Nolin, "Urban Parks in Sweden at the Turn of the Twentieth Century," in *Public Nature: Scenery, History and Park Design*, ed. Ethan Carr, Shaun Eyring, and Richard Wilson (Charlottesville, VA: University of Virginia Press, 2013), 115–24.

2 In addition to the planning of parks near new housing projects, allotment gardens also allayed discomfort with urban life. See Catharina Nolin, "Koloniträdgårdensrörelsen i Stockholm," in *Stadens odlare*, ed. Christina Westergren (Stockholm, Sweden: Nordiska museets förlag, 2003).

3 Constant observes that this project by Asplund was likely influenced by Lewerentz's design of an entry sequence for the Rud Cemetery near Karlstad of May 1918. See Constant 1994, 54.

4 This could be a representation of Yggdrasil, a tree from Norse cosmology. A Swedish version of this tree grew next to the original temple at Gamla Upsalla. See Adam von Bremen, *History of The Archbishops of Hamburg-Bremen* (New York: Columbia University Press, 1959).

5 See Uvedale Price, *An Essay on the Picturesque, as Compared with the Sublime and Beautiful; and on the Use of Studying Pictures, for the Purpose of Improving Real Landscape* (London: J. Robson, 1797).

6 Nineteen twenty-one is the official date of the sculpture in the *catalogue raisonné* of the works of Milles. Correspondence of Milles at the National Library of Sweden (Kungliga Biblioteket) could reveal more about his collaboration with Asplund.

7 This information was given to the author by Hedvig Schönbäck of the Stockholm City Museum. At the invitation of the Cemetery Authority in 1995, historians at the museum conducted a thorough documentation of the Woodland Cemetery.

8 Correspondence with Hedvig Schönbäck, historian at the Stockholm City Museum.

9 A style of furniture that prevailed at the time of King Gustav III (r. 1771–92). See H. Arnold Barton, *Essays on Scandanavian History* (Carbondale, IL: Southern Illinois University Press, 2009).

10 According to Hedvig Schönbäck, this painting was stolen a number of years ago.

References

Andersson, Thorbjörn. 1993. "Erik Glemme and the Stockholm Park System." In *Modern Landscape Architecture: A Critical Review*, edited by Marc Treib, 114–33. Cambridge, MA: MIT Press.

——. 1998. "The Functionalism of Gardening Art." In *Sweden: Twentieth Century Architecture*, edited by Claes Caldenby, Jöran Lindvall, and Wilfried Wang, 226–41. Munich, Germany: Prestel.

Bergson, Henri. 1911. *Creative Evolution*. New York: Henry Holt.

Carlsson, Sten. 1989. "The Transformation of Swedish Society." In *Tradition and Modern Society*, edited by Sven Gustavsson, 19–26. Stockholm, Sweden: Almqvist & Wiksell.

Constant, Caroline. 1994. *The Woodland Cemetery: Towards a Spiritual Landscape*. Stockholm, Sweden: Byggförlaget.

Cornell, Elias. 1986. "The Sky as a Vault." In *Asplund*, edited by Claes Caldenby and Olof Hultin, 23–33. New York: Rizzoli.

Eriksson, Eva. 1998. "International Impulses and the National Tradition." In *Sweden: Twentieth Century Architecture*, edited by Claes Caldenby, Jöran Lindvall, and Wilfried Wang, 18–45. Munich, Germany: Prestel 1998.

Facos, Michelle. 1998. *Nationalism and the Nordic Imagination*. Berkeley, CA: University of California Press.

Johansson, Bengt. 1996. *Tallum: Gunnar Asplund's and Sigurd Lewerentz's Woodland Cemetery in Stockholm*. Stockholm, Sweden: Byggförlaget.

Jones, Peter Blundell. 2006. *Gunnar Asplund*. London: Phaidon Press.

Kåberg, Helena. 2008. "An Introduction to Gregor Paulsson's *Better Things for Everday Life*." In *Modern Swedish Design: Three Founding Texts*, edited by Lucy Creagh, Helena Kåberg, and Barbara Miller Lane, 58–71. New York: Museum of Modern Art.

Key, Ellen. 2008. "Beauty in the Home." In *Modern Swedish Design: Three Founding Texts*, edited by Lucy Creagh, Helena Kåberg, and Barbara Miller Lane, 32–57. New York: Museum of Modern Art.

Morris, Richard. 2006. "Death on Display." In *Rhetorics of Display*, edited by Lawrence Prelli, 204–27. Columbia, SC: University of South Carolina Press.

Nilsson, Lars. 2006. "Stockholm and Green Space: An Introduction." In *The European City and Green Space*, edited by Peter Clark, 99–110. Aldershot, UK: Ashgate.

Nolin, Catharina. 2006. "Stockholm's Urban Parks: Meeting Places and Social Contexts from 1860–1930." In *The European City and Greenspace*, edited by Peter Clark, 111–26. Aldershot, UK: Ashgate.

Ruth, Arne. 1984. "The Second New Nation: The Mythology of Modern Sweden." *Daedalus* 113: 53–96.

Sernander, Rutger. 1926. *Stockholms Natur*. Uppsala, Sweden: Almqvist & Wiksells Forläg.

Wrede, Stuart. 1980. *The Architecture of Erik Gunnar Asplund*. Cambridge, MA: MIT Press.

3

OBSERVATORIELUNDEN AND STADSBIBLIOTEKET

Intensifying the present

Public libraries of the early twentieth century in America had a grand public mission. Though often funded by plutocrats, they were dedicated to opening opportunity to anyone with curiosity and a will towards self-improvement. Like railroad stations and museums, they were conceived as public amenities akin to the baths in ancient Rome. For most at the time, classicism was appropriate for an institution intended to nurture ambition and good citizenship. As part of the City Beautiful movement, which followed in the wake of the Chicago Exhibition of 1893, every developing city in America wanted a plan that would compose new public institutions in a context of Roman grandeur. Invariably, in the Beaux Arts tradition, favored designs had a Parisian quality, with broad avenues, reflecting pools, and flowing fountains. Libraries, in particular, were sited to command these grand public spaces and assume their place of importance among seats of government.

Though geographically removed from Western Europe, Stockholm was not immune to this mania for civic grandeur and progressive reforms. The form it took, however, was decidedly different. Instead of a majestic structure that commands an axis or square, the Stockholm Public Library, or Stadsbiblioteket, sits at a major intersection, next to a steep hill. Contrary to familiar Beaux Arts practice, the library design by Asplund makes no attempt to dominate the surrounding park, called Observatorielunden, also designed by Asplund. Instead, park and library exist as two parallel experiences of landscape and architecture. A visitor is quietly challenged to make connections between parts of the landscape as well as between landscape and architecture. This requires an act of attentive reading that can shift meanings depending on weather, mood, or approach.

It is fair to ask what values related to education lie behind this dialogue between landscape and architecture. In the United States, Carrère and Hastings and their peers were attempting to translate a widely held vision of the classical world and

Renaissance humanism to the modern city. Those who founded the grand public libraries in North America no doubt shared this vision as well as a nationalist purpose to form their version of good citizens. From the evidence of landscapes and buildings, Asplund and his contemporaries had a distinctly different conception of the ancient world and the good citizen that derived from the philosophy of Friedrich Nietzsche and Nordic classicists of the nineteenth century. This contributed to a different form of humanism that sought to explain the present by revealing origins from the ancient world and by reconciling the inner life and the outside world.

As a prelude to explaining this humanism, it is important to know that the Stadsbibliotek was not the first public institution in Stockholm to favor relationships with the natural world over those with the city. When the City of Stockholm selected Ragnar Östberg in 1907 to design a new Town Hall, he was more interested in a monumental presence that would command Lake Mälaren and reflect well in the water (Figure 3.1). Östberg was also interested in relating to existing landforms, though this may be less apparent to the visitor. Referring to the new Town Hall, he wrote that "[t]he building, in fact, stands on the outskirts of a rocky promontory which, running from the above mentioned ridge, "Kungsklippan," in the northwest, dips down precipitously, carrying the lofty tower on its extreme south-east point" (Östberg 1929, 23).

Though Östberg eschewed classicism in favor of a Nordic vernacular, he still intended to make vast ceremonial spaces that would lend a sacred gravity to civic life. He created this sacred quality through a blending of Christian planning and nature worship. For example, his Golden Room is a processional space that concludes with an enormous mosaic of Queen Mälaren, goddess of the lake.

FIGURE 3.1 Stockholm Town Hall, Ragnar Östberg, 1911–23

Source: The Swedish Center for Architecture and Design, ARKM.1962-101-1037b

Despite this grandeur, his floor plans have a willful eccentricity, distorting an otherwise rectilinear courtyard to conform possibly to the natural conditions of the shoreline. This enormous court, opening to Lake Mälaren through a generous open portico, allows the outdoors to sweep into the building. In addition, the parterre garden that occupies the space between the Town Hall and the water has carefully selected statuary that celebrates Stockholm heroes and villains such as Birger Jarl and the god Loki (Figure 3.2) and immortalizes the sacred log that gave Stockholm its name.[1] Overall, Östberg achieved a monumentality that is detached from everyday urbanism and more closely engaged with the natural world. Furthermore, he succeeded in giving city government the status of a sacred cult with vast ceremonial spaces. Finally, he effectively used a garden to tell ancient stories that anchor the new civic institution to the place.

This tendency to locate fundamental meanings in the natural world can also be found in a school of Swedish landscape painting from the late nineteenth and early twentieth centuries known as National Romanticism, mentioned previously. Many young painters had returned from long stays in France and Germany, eager to define a particular Swedish sensibility towards landscape (Facos 1998, 27–45). One priority was to demonstrate how natural scenes have the power to immediately evoke or reflect states of mind. Prince Eugen's *The Forest* is the most famous example of this genre, playing on both the Swedish attachment to the forest as a dwelling place and an implied melancholy (Figure 3.3). Another genre, represented by J. A. G. Acke, was meant to show the analogy between the power and grace of the human body and the forms and forces of Nature. His painting *Salt, Wind, and Sea* reflects this formula, showing male nudes posed on rocks with crashing waves in the bright sun. A third tendency aimed to reveal how Swedish cultural rituals—particularly Midsummer's Eve—have the unique capacity to blend sensuality and nature worship. Anders Zorn's *Midsummer Dance* is an exemplar of this purpose, displaying dancing peasants in traditional costume on the eve of the solstice; by tradition social taboos at this time are relaxed so all senses might be used to capture the moment (Figure 3.4).

Another contribution of National Romanticism was a reconsideration of traditional buildings through painting. Unlike Skansen, Artur Hazelius's museum of traditional buildings in Stockholm, these paintings portray how ancient buildings relate to landscape in specific ways. Richard Bergh's *Vision, Scene from Visby*, for example, draws attention to visual associations between fortress walls, undulating landscape, trees, and ships (Figure 3.5). Karl Nordström's *The Neighboring Farm* points out the relationship between two long farmhouses and the horizon of the sea (Figure 3.6). Finally, Prince Eugen's *The Old Castle* teaches a lesson of contrast, showing how a simple white building can make the viewer more aware of the gentle curve of the landscape and the Baroque majesty of a cloud form (Figure 3.7). All of these paintings suggest that human (or Swedish) presence is very much part of the natural world as an enhancement rather than an intrusion. Unlike the familiar Western cultural pattern, explained by Philippe Descola (2013, 54), where the wilder parts of natural world are seen as alien and dangerous, Swedes prefer

FIGURE 3.2 Stockholm Town Hall garden, Ragnar Östberg

Source: The Swedish Center for Architecture and Design, ARKM.1962-102-173

FIGURE 3.3
Prince Eugen, *The Forest*, sketch, 1892

Source: Prins EugensWaldemarsudde

FIGURE 3.4
Anders Zorn, *Midsummer Dance*, 1897

Source: Photo © Nationalmuseum, Stockholm

to think of themselves as very much at home in dark forests, ragged coastlines, and high mountains.

This search for meaning in landscape and latent anti-urbanism can also be found in the thinking of Rutger Sernander, mentioned previously. He was a professor of botany at Uppsala University, concerned about the growth of Stockholm in the early twentieth century and the need to preserve exceptional features of the landscape within the city, particularly groves of older trees and wilder outcrops. He campaigned for a new kind of city park that would protect these places in a relatively raw state and make them accessible to new housing estates that were growing on the periphery (Andersson 1993, 118). In 1926, he published a book called *Stockholms Natur* that presented a number of natural sites, mainly groves and trees, as urban landmarks on a par with monuments in other European cities (Sernander 1926) (Figure 3.8). Swedes, in his terms, should not seek nationalism and civic identity in the usual forms of urban design typical of North America and Western Europe. Instead, they should find it in trees, outcrops, and bodies of water. Important buildings, meanwhile, were left to rely on their identification with these features for significance.

The site selected by the library commission for a new public library fits the description of one of Sernander's urban landmarks (Figure 3.9). Though located at a significant intersection between Sveavägen and Odengatan in the Vasastan neighborhood, it was also at the base of a significant promontory called Observatoriekullen. This hill was part of an esker called the Brunkebergsåsen, a long ridge

FIGURE 3.5 Richard Bergh, *Vision: Scene from Visby*, 1894

Source: Photo © Nationalmuseum, Stockholm

FIGURE 3.6 Karl Nordström, *The Neighboring Farm*, 1894

Source: Photo © Nationalmuseum, Stockholm

FIGURE 3.7 Prince Eugen, *The Old Castle*, 1893

Source: Per Myrehed photo, Prins Eugens Waldemarsudde

FIGURE 3.8 Prince Eugen's Oak at Prins Eugens Waldemarsudde

Source: Rutger Sernander, *Stockholms Natur*, Stockholm: Almqvist & Wiksell, 1926

made of sand and gravel that was left by a streambed within a glacier (Figure 3.10). Because of the difficulty of making east/west streets, it had been dramatically erased and eroded over centuries. It is more noteworthy in modern history as the site of the Stockholm Observatory, built in 1753. Though it became obsolete as an observatory in the early twentieth century, it has continued as a museum of astronomy and more recently as a restaurant. Despite the central location at the intersection of two major streets, in the early twentieth century the Observatoriekullen had been neglected for decades and was used primarily by a gravel business.

In addition to a consensus about the value of the natural world in urban life, Swedes also had a deep-seated egalitarian tradition. Because of widespread concern about growing emigration to the United States, great efforts were made in the early twentieth century to modernize the economy and to make opportunities more accessible to the common man.[2] The public library committee's mission could be seen as part of this broader effort. In particular, they were guided by the work of Valfrid Palmgren, a prominent thinker in education, who wrote a book in 1909 called *Libraries and Public Education: Notes from Student Travel to the United States*. Her research established her as a public figure and led to a position on the Stockholm City Council. Her great cause was to found libraries that would be open to all, free of charge and removed from political or religious interference. In particular, she was committed to establishing reading rooms and collections designed for the needs of children. Most of these reforms she learned from libraries in the United States and were recorded in her book about her research trip.

Though the Stockholm City Council was committed to her principles, the actual planning and construction of the library required a long gestation. After a Public Library Committee was formed in 1910, a modest proposal for a new library was made in 1912. It was clearly underfunded, and in response, the Wallenberg family made a gift in 1918 that launched the project (Constant 1989, 54). Soon after, the city donated the site at Observatory Hill and Asplund was appointed by the Committee for the Stockholm City Library to assist in planning for the library and to research library innovations in Europe and the United States.[3] Following the precepts of Valfrid Palmgren, they were interested in space planning that would allow more access to the stacks by users and dedicated space for children's activities and collections.

Initially there was a larger planning agenda for this district that went beyond a site for a public library. Asplund had previously been part of a planning committee for this part of the city before he was hired by the Library Committee in 1920 to prepare a competition brief. Soon after this, he received the commission for the library itself (Jones 2006, 111). University faculty buildings, including those for economics and sciences, were to be located in this area. His earliest site plans from 1919 reflect this program, and a more refined version of 1922 maintains it. Here the hill was given two characters, a terraced slope on the north and west sides and a picturesque landscape with a spiral path on the south (Figure 3.11). The terraces were to be made with ranges of buildings, and the summit was to be crowned

FIGURE 3.9 Stadsbiblioteket location map

Source: Author drawing after Det Centrala Stockholm 1948, published by Generalstabens litografiska anstalt, Stockholm, 1948, National Library of Sweden, Maps and Pictures, KoB 3 a

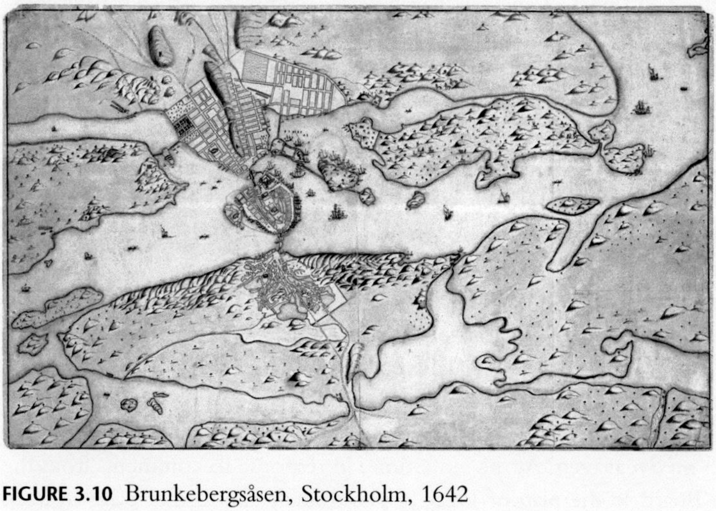

FIGURE 3.10 Brunkebergsåsen, Stockholm, 1642

Source: National Library of Sweden, Maps and Pictures, Stockholm 51:30 nr 187

with a university building with an open court connected to cylinder-shaped building, also with an open court. Two grand axial sequences were made to ascend to the summit from Sveavägen. One of these was received by the courtyard building while the other terminated at the circular building, the site of the former observatory. The ascent from Odengaten, in the area of steep open terraces, required switchback ramps that reached the plateau in a passage outside the rectangular building. The library, cast as the worldly introduction to the more rarefied plane of higher education, is sited along Sveavägen, bordering an entry plaza at the corner. Initially, the library was conceived as a square with a domed rotunda in the middle. After a model was presented for the first version of this plan in 1919 (see Figure 3.11), a newspaper called it "an Academic Acropolis" (Eriksson 2008, 61) In addition to the important view from library plaza to hill, two other primary intentions can be seen in this plan. One concerns the treatment of the hill in both architectural and pastoral themes, represented by the circle and square.[4] The other relates to the capacity of the library to embody both as it resolves both circle and square.

The City Design Board objected to the density of university buildings and expressed a preference for exposing more of the hill to surrounding streets. As a result, this scheme was revised again in 1923 (Bergsten 1923, 307). The old observatory now shared a broad plateau with a square courtyard building, and the library was moved to the west side of the corner square along Odengaten (Figure 3.12). The corner of Sveavägen and Odengatan again was left as an open plaza, but the library was moved to border Odengatan. This plaza allowed a gracious forecourt to the library and a direct view to the top of the hill, one of Asplund's primary considerations. The School of Economics, later designed by Ivor Tengbom, was sited further south on Sveavägen, separated from the corner plaza by a long public garden. The slopes of the hill, meanwhile, were reconstructed to accommodate plantings and curving pathways. The City Design Board had objections to the new plaza design in 1923, wanting the library sited at the corner of Sveavägen and Odengatan. Asplund argued against this, expressing concern about maintaining the view of the hill from the corner (Eriksson 2008, 61).

In 1924, Asplund won a competition for a park along Sveavägen. Over the course of a decade, he refined this design with many versions to arrive at the design of the park that exists today. According to the plan of 1923, the top of the hill is marked by a small plaza, while Sveavägen is bordered by a park with a long reflecting pool. Soon after, in 1926, he also made an unbuilt proposal for a market hall along Odengatan with a formal garden on the roof (Eriksson 2008, 58). This was on the site of an existing open-air market that still persists today. At this time, the library was also presented with its distinctive skew, a slight dislocation from the street grid that allows an entrance to the reflecting pool park further south on Sveavägen. At the same time, in response to comments from the City Design Board to the plan of 1923, Asplund made the former plaza in front of the library into a plinth occupied by shops below and plaza above. This plinth is bisected by a stepped ramp that leads to the entrance of the library.

FIGURE 3.11 "Academic Acropolis" plan and model of 1919, Asplund

Source: The Swedish Center for Architecture and Design, ARKM.1984-05-10, ARKM.1988-104-0384

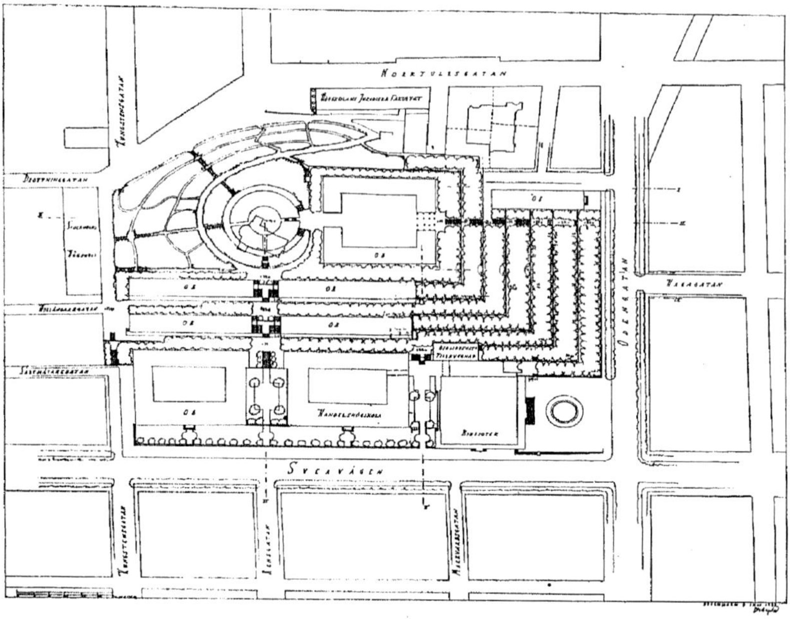

E. G. ASPLUND. FÖRSLAG TILL OBSERVATORIEHÖJDENS ORDNANDE 1922

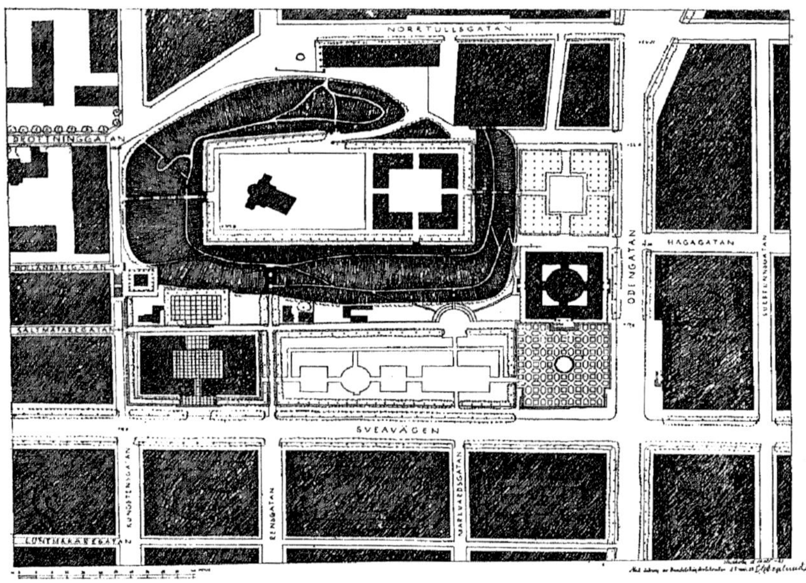

E. G. ASPLUND. FÖRSLAG TILL OBSERVATORIEHÖJDENS ORDNANDE 1923

FIGURE 3.12 Observatorielunden site plans of 1922 and 1923, Asplund

Source: Carl Bergsten, "Stockholm Stadsbiblioteks Förläggning," *Byggmastären* 1923, 305–08

Once the location of the library was firmly determined, Asplund produced several plans of Observatorielunden from 1929 through 1930 that show different versions of a continuous chute of water that would connect a viewing terrace with the reflecting pool below. This was a way to assure a visual and possibly narrative connection between hill and reflecting pool. At first, this watercourse was shown simply as a straight line from the terrace to the pool. In later versions from 1930 the terrace is placed higher while the watercourse, beginning in a square fountain, is placed immediately to the south and segmented into a straight run and a curved one. In one version this terrace is far more extensive than previous ones with formal flower gardens and a grove of cut trees at the viewing platform (Figure 3.13).[5] One of Asplund's associates related how a model was built of one of these versions to simulate the action of the water (Engfors 1990, 24). This may have led them to adopt a simpler solution in the final version where a meandering stream emerges out of a grotto, positioned lower in the hill.[6]

Though it is impossible to reconstruct exactly Asplund's reasoning behind these alternatives for Observatorielunden, there is a clear shift from an architectural landscape that transforms from library to hilltop (see Figure 3.11) to a scheme featuring a duality between hill and library, to borrow Eva Eriksson's term (2008, 58). In the earlier scheme, visitors would see the architectural imprint of the library as garden and courtyard building and perhaps arrive at the conclusion that the qualities of all of these spaces underlie the library. In the second, visitors would be encouraged to contrast the experience of the library's rotunda with the experience at the top of observatory hill. The final version, which likely dates to 1934, revisits this contrast of the hilltop and the library's rotunda (Figure 3.14). In this case, the observatory is preserved in addition to a lower terrace that can easily be seen from below. What is different is that there is no longer a direct ascent to the top of the hill; the winding pathways are the only means. Here, the library's rotunda is approached by stairs inside the library and stairs that carve into a podium outside the library (Figure 3.15). This is analogous to the ascent by stairs from Sveavägen to the cylinder-shaped building in the 1919 plan and model. In other words, the library has its own ascent to a simulated hilltop experience. The hill itself, meanwhile, is treated as picturesque landscape with winding paths that slowly ascend to the plateau at the top. These are, in effect, two parallel sequences intended to provoke close comparison.

One possible reading of building and landscape begins with the foyer of the library building. The foyer is a pause midway in the sequence from sidewalk to rotunda (see Figure 3.15). You ascend a long-stepped ramp to the entrance of the library, which is a gigantic keyhole with a light curtain wall as the barrier (Figure 3.16), suggesting that the large opening is intended to invite the outside in. The scale of the gigantic opening was originally contrasted with small sculptural handles of Adam and Eve by Nils Sögren on the front door (Figure 3.17). Just inside the door, at eye level, are murals of the *Iliad* by Ivar Johnsson done in black plaster. They illustrate the death of Patroklos and the revenge of Achilles (Figure 3.18). An obvious first assumption is that these scenes have specific moral content that the architect

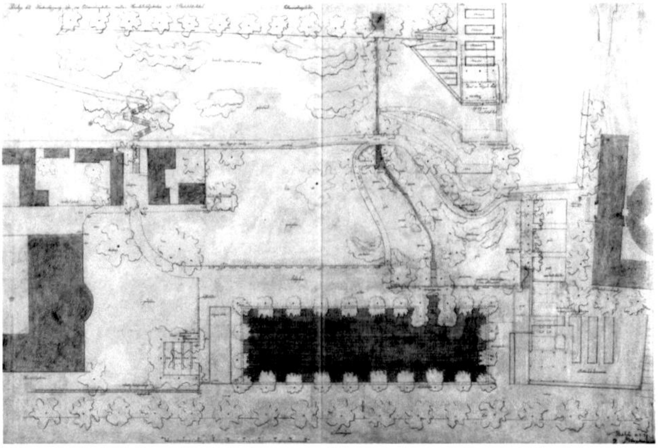

FIGURE 3.13
Observatorielunden schematic plan, 1930, Asplund

Source: The Swedish Center for Architecture and Design, ARKM. 1988-02-7700 H

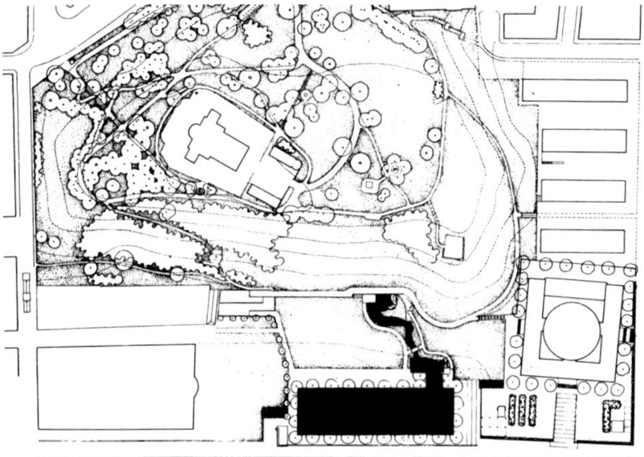

FIGURE 3.14
Final plan of Observatorielunden circa 1934, Asplund

Source: G. Holmdahl, S. Lind., K. Ödeen (eds), *Gunnar Asplund Architect*, Stockholm, Sweden: A. B. Tibskriften Byggmästaren, 1950

wants to deliver before visitors proceed up the stairs to the rotunda. A second reading might suggest that these scenes were intended as a representation of the first story with a known author in the Western tradition.[7] In effect, Asplund may want us to be mindful of origins where a narrative that derives from particular landscapes became enshrined as a book in our cultural tradition. In reference to the figures of Adam and Eve, meanwhile, one might speculate that they are a companion narrative where knowledge is a curse, punished by exclusion from Eden. Alternatively, they can be seen as another first story that comes from an oral tradition. Finally, as Wrede suggests, these figures can be seen as "an insistent reminder of the flesh to those delving into the world of the mind" (Wrede 1980, 123).

Another possibility suggests that the *Iliad* is a reference to interest in pre-Homeric civilization pursued by many German scholars in the nineteenth century, particularly Friedrich Nietzsche. For these humanists, "Homer could give a picture of the human mind" (Porter 2004, 14). There was some concern, however, about what could be found there. "The Homeric psyche could represent either an early

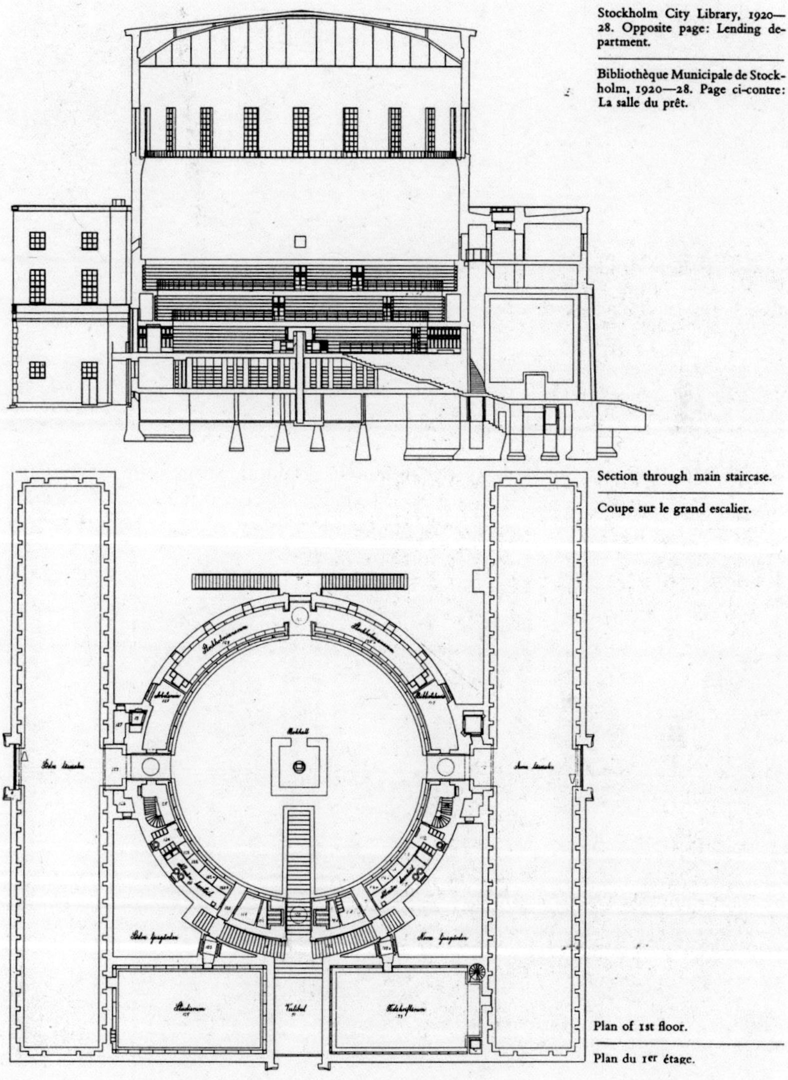

FIGURE 3.15 Section and first floor plans of Stadsbiblioteket

Source: G. Holmdahl, S. Lind., K. Ödeen (eds), *Gunnar Asplund Architect*, Stockholm, Sweden: A. B. Tibskriften Byggmästaren, 1950

FIGURE 3.16 Ramp at Stadsbiblioteket entrance, Asplund, Stockholm, 1928–30

Source: Author photo

FIGURE 3.17 Adam and Eve door handles at entrance, Nils Sögren

Source: Herbert Lindgren photo, Stockholm City Museum, FG 8907

FIGURE 3.18 Stadsbiblioteket foyer, Asplund, 1921–28

Source: The Swedish Center for Architecture and Design, ARKM.1985-109-151

and superceded instance of the universal self (as it were, an imperfect and undeveloped version of the self) or a lost ideal of selfhood, one untainted by the ills of civilization and especially of modern life, that may or—more frequently—may not be reattained in the modern present" (14–15).

In addition to differences of opinion about the significance of the Homeric psyche, there was also different thinking about the relevance of the past. Some classical scholars, such as Wilamowitz, insisted that the past is "an objectively separate entity"; skeptics would go further and claim that because of this separateness, it has no relevance.[8] A third version advocated an aestheticization of the past in the manner of Winckelmann (Hamilton 2004, 58). In contrast, Nietzsche and his followers promoted a construction of the past based on continuity, where the past cannot be escaped. The only way to properly understand the present, in fact, is through study of the past. "A very precise retrospective analysis will lead us to the realization that we are the multiplication of many pasts" (Emden 2004, 387).

Even when a consensus exists about the significance of the past, allowances must be made for two concepts of time. One is linear historical time, which "is based on an inability to actively forget; this time is marked by *ressentiment*, the inward turning of suffering, a pathos" (Stern 2007, 52). The other is circular time, when "elements of the past are addressed in the moment in order to create a metaphor of self" (52). In the life of the individual, the first kind of time is notable for an identification with the past, and, in Nietzsche's terms, it is distinctly unhealthy. Circular time, in contrast, is a matter of "active forgetting" and a willful recreation of the past to suit the needs of the moment; this is a state of health. It is the coexistence of these two kinds of time "that activates the Nietzschean idea of tragedy as the collision of competing narratives" (52). This creative activity associated with circular time could be seen as what Nietzsche would call "a philology that can teach us how to be *untimely*" (Hamilton 2004, 58), or how to "intensify the present into the monstrous and the eternal" (58).

This could be seen as Asplund's ultimate intention in designing a sequence that takes the visitor past Adam and Eve figures and bas-reliefs of the *Iliad*. This is a genealogical moment, in Nietzsche's terms, where the visitor is presented with dual origins, one Homeric and the other biblical. The choice to continue up the stairs to encounter a world of books is a creative act, a version of circular time where choices are made to construct a self. One on hand, there is the fate, or acceptance, of cultural origins, of which nationalism is a part; on the other, there is the possibility of "an affirmation of chance and becoming" (Stern 2007, 53). This thesis is supported by Asplund's original plan for a mosaic in the floor of the foyer, copied from one that he had seen in Rome, which shows a skeleton on a bed of spikes who points to the expression "Know thyself."

Once the visitor arrives in the rotunda, there is a panoramic view of terraces of books, with signs to indicate different languages and a view upward into the lofty space (Figure 3.19). In addition to the implied cosmic reference, this room was designed to make the collection immediately legible to the user. Originally,

FIGURE 3.19 Stadsbiblioteket rotunda, Asplund, 1921–28

Source: Author photo

Asplund conceived the roof of this space as a dome. Because it is more difficult to make a dome into a visible landmark and the complications involved with making functional skylights, he abandoned the dome in favor of a tall drum that would still suggest an infinite vault of the sky. Curiously, the inner wall is rough, with a repeating pattern of subtly articulated stones covered with plaster. One theory is that this texture was intended by Asplund to resemble clouds.[9]

Before or after using the library, patrons will invariably take the opportunity to visit Observatorielunden, the park that surrounds the library to the south and west (Figure 3.20). Asplund alludes to the park with a distinctive drinking fountain in the library, located next to a second-story window that overlooks the reflecting pool. The park can roughly be divided into two parts, a large reflecting pool surrounded by willows and the hill itself, including the ascending paths to a plateau at the top. Whereas the Garden of Eden was only implied at Asplund's Skandia Cinema, here he has a chance to realize a tranquil idyll. He casts this spell primarily through the mirror-like qualities of the reflecting pool and the flanking willows. These are the trees that would grow well next to a pond or stream in the natural world, and they are represented here in a civic context. Unlike the waterside parterre garden at the Town Hall, which derives its themes from a building, this is not a library garden. There are no sculptures that immortalize the literary life, and the library, though it has a veiled presence, does not command this space.

Ivar Tengbom's School of Economics, located immediately south of the reflecting pool, enjoys a more conventional axial relationship with this park (see Figure 3.14). By virtue of a small concrete pavilion with a flat roof, however, sited at the south end of the reflecting pool, Asplund makes it clear that this building is not the sponsor of this space. This very modern structure serves multiple purposes to introduce the garden. For those arriving on foot from the south, it initially acts as a viewing device that frames the rotunda of the library above and a view of the reflecting pool below (Figure 3.21). The lower view centers on a hallow plinth, occupied by a restaurant that acts as a forecourt to the library above. This plinth, included as part of the last phase of the library's construction, was designed in the Functionalist style with continuous windows from the ground to a nine-foot height. It is noteworthy that the concrete pavilion and the plinth are Asplund's first Functionalist creations and are works of *garden* architecture. They make no pretense about the active expression of machine production. Instead, they use structural technology to address a difficult formal agenda in a garden and to impart a light and ethereal quality.

At the north end of the garden, the slight skew of the library makes an entrance to the park, quietly inviting those who pass by to walk on the other side of the wall (Figure 3.22). The skew also accentuates the presence of the library as a mass that is seen obliquely. For those entering at the south end, the entrance is marked by the concrete pavilion, mentioned previously, that both frames an initial view of the reflecting pool and shelters a sculpture by Nils Möllerberg of a nude female called *Youth* (Figure 3.23). This figure, without any obvious narrative content, is meant to set the tone of this place and invite you to make your own story.

FIGURE 3.20 View of reflecting pool from south, Observatorielunden, Asplund, 1921–34

Source: The Swedish Center for Architecture and Design, ARKM.1985-109-135

FIGURE 3.21 Pavilion at reflecting pool, Observatorielunden, Asplund, 1928–34

Source: Author photo

FIGURE 3.22 North entry at reflecting pool, Observatorielunden, Asplund, 1928–34

Source: Author photo

FIGURE 3.23 Diagonal view with *Youth* by Nils Möllerberg, Observatorielunden, Asplund, 1928–34

Source: Author photo

A shapely nude woman in a bathing position, willow trees, and a reflecting pool can take you a number of places in your imagination. A Greek myth may come to mind, or you might simply allow yourself greater sensual awareness as you linger in the park. In any case, the sculpture is life-sized and placed on a low wall at sitting height. Invariably people sit next to the sculpture, so this figure, whether mythological or not, is seen in the context of everyday bodies and commonplace activity. It can be seen as part of Asplund's practice to place art at places of arrival to pose questions and to set a tone.

If you chose to sit down on the benches that flank the pool, this invitation to take an interest in others is quietly reinforced. Here, you will more than likely look directly across the pool at another visitor on a bench, framed by willows. Should you be facing Sveavägen, you will also see the heads above the wall of those passing on the sidewalk. On a summer day, there are few if any rules here; small children bathe nude and dogs splash freely. The low slope to the west, at the base of the hill, is used like a beach where groups and couples recline on the grass (Figure 3.24). In early summer, at the end of the school term, when large trucks drive by full of recent graduates, dancing wildly, the sculpture near the pool called *Dancing Youth* by Ivar Johnsson appears strangely appropriate (Figure 3.25).

From this vantage point, a part of the top of the hill is quite visible thanks to an open visual corridor that frames a sculpture, seen in silhouette. If you decide to ascend the hill, contrary to earlier designs with axial routes, the hill cannot be climbed by a straight path. You have the option to go left or right to follow two different paths that slowly ascend the hill (see Figure 3.14). If you happen to have visited the library already, it is possible that you will be reminded of the two curving staircases to the rotunda. If you depart from the reflecting pool, one route

FIGURE 3.24 Lawn near reflecting pool, Observatorielunden, Asplund, 1928–34

Source: Author photo

FIGURE 3.25 *Dancing Youth* by Ivar Johnsson, 1937

Source: Author photo

allows you to walk along a meandering stream, created by Asplund, which has its source in a small stone grotto (Figure 3.26). At that point, you can go left or right to ascend the hill. The path to the right takes you around to the rear of the library and a steep staircase. The path on the left, cut into the hillside with a battered granite retaining wall, heads toward the south and the School of Economics. Taking this route, you arrive very soon at a turning point where there is a bench and a framed view of St. Johannes Church to the southeast (Figure 3.27). Because the center of Stockholm has not allowed high-rise buildings, churches and landforms are still significant landmarks. St. Engelbrekt's Church, for example, later terminates a view towards the east from the summit.

Once you arrive almost to the top of the hill, coming from the south you pass the observatory, now a restaurant. Soon after, you arrive at the edge of the precipice where there are large benches with shade and an open view to the reflecting pool below and a view of the city towards the east (Figure 3.28). Further along this path is a small trapezoidal plaza with a large sculpture of the centaur Chiron, called *Kentauren*, in the far corner (Figure 3.29). This is the same sculpture that was seen

FIGURE 3.26
Grotto at source of stream, Observatorielunden, Asplund, 1924–34

Source: Author photo

FIGURE 3.27
View of St. Johannes's Church, Observatorielunden, Asplund, 1924–34

Source: Author photo

FIGURE 3.28
View of reflecting pool from Observatoriekullen, Asplund, 1924–34

Source: Author photo

FIGURE 3.29 *Kentauren* by Sigrid Fridman, Observatorielunden, 1939

Source: Author photo

from below as the marker of your destination (see Figure 3.25). The path orients a view of the rotunda of the library immediately behind the statue.

For some, it will require some research to discover all of the meanings associated with Chiron. As hybrids of men and nature, centaurs were wild elements in Greek mythology. Chiron, however, was notable for his exceptional wisdom and self-control. He was the educator of the gods and resided in a cave on the top of Mount Pelion. Among others, he advised Peleus about how to catch the water nymph Thetis, who became his wife. Their son Achilles became the pupil of Chiron. Though presumably immortal, Chiron chose to end his life after being accidentally wounded by a poisoned arrow from Heracles. He is immortalized in the constellation Sagittarius, or the Archer. Given this eclectic history, this figure could be seen to function as a link between the existing observatory and the library's educational mission. In a secondary way, it makes some association with the life of Achilles portrayed in the *Iliad* and the foyer of the library.

This sculpture is also linked in a more ambiguous way to the sculpture on the edge of the reflecting pool immediately below it. An open visual corridor orients the view from one sculpture to the other, with St. Engelbrekt's Church in the distance (Figure 3.30). The stream, in addition, runs for part of this route from its origin in the grotto (see Figure 3.14). Because of this axial association, it is reasonable to expect the narrative related to Chiron to continue. I was anticipating that the figures below would portray Thetis and Peleus, the parents of Achilles. In fact, Asplund originally considered sculptures that appear to be mythological figures, possibly Actaeon, Chiron's protégé, and Artemis.[10] Instead, the selected sculpture of nude figures dancing, previously mentioned, is not specific about any particular identity or association (see Figure 3.25). Likewise, the sculpture of the bathing woman at the end of the reflecting pool, also previously mentioned, is equally nonspecific (see Figure 3.23). It is clear that at a certain point Asplund abandoned any clear narrative intention in favor of a more open-ended form of expression.

This change in perspective is reflected in Asplund's shifting opinion about the sculpture on the hill. He initially approved of Sigrid Fridman's sculpture of Chiron when it was originally proposed in 1930 as a maquette. Later, however, he changed his mind when the sculptures next the reflecting pool were selected with no clear narrative. He feared in 1938 that the *Kentauren* sculpture would be an imposition on the tranquil idyll of the reflecting pool. Despite his protest, the City Design Board insisted on the installation of Fridman's sculpture (Johanson 1948, 97). What some may assume to be a design process carefully controlled by Asplund was not. Instead the complete garden reveals his hesitations, his development, and the occasional intervention of the public authorities.

This description of a visit to the library and park is meant to show an intention to create a network of relationships, using calculated views, sculptures as focal points and contrasting sequences. Though the setting is completely different, Asplund attempted to set up an analogous conversation between parts at the Skandia Cinema (1922–23) on Drottninggatan, a number of blocks south of

FIGURE 3.30 Visual corridor from hilltop to reflecting pool, Observatorielunden, Asplund 1924–34

Source: Author photo

Observatoriekullen. Here, the visitor is presented with a layering of readings that include a matter-of-fact understanding of a cinema, an Italian town, a night sky, and figures of Adam and Eve (Figure 3.31). For those willing to make the effort, there is an invitation to ask how these seemingly disparate elements might relate to each other. Those who make the trip to the top of Observatoriekullen are put into a similar position. Here, they are presented with a beautiful panoramic view of Stockholm, the large rotunda of the library, and an open view of the reflecting pool with willows below. At this elevation it is possible to see the frieze of two repeated symbols surrounding the library's rotunda. According to Ewa Andersson, one is the harp for higher learning, while the other is the wing for commerce.[11] Asplund apparently saw the library as a union of these two pursuits. The view from Observatoriekullen invites the same kind of hybrid thinking, though in different terms. The commanding view can be seen as an analogy for the power and detachment of higher learning, while the pond and dancing figures below are a reminder of sensual pleasures of all kinds. Whatever wisdom or insight may come from a library could be seen as a reconciliation of these impulses.

This interpretation is offered as one plausible example; the only certainty here is that Asplund deliberately places the visitor in the position of reader, where there is active participation rather than passive acceptance. According to Wolfgang Iser, it is "the convergence of text and reader" that brings the literary work into existence in a virtual world somewhere between the text and the mind of the reader. He sees reading as a process of anticipation and retrospection, and sentences build on one another to create a constantly shifting meaning. "Each intentional sentence correlative," he writes, "opens up a particular horizon, which is modified, if not completely changed, by succeeding sentences" (Iser 1974, 278). Narratives, he claims, that make everything perfectly clear and make no demands on the imagination of the reader are inherently boring. In this respect, the biggest challenge comes from deliberate gaps in the text, more obvious in contemporary fiction, that require the reader to knit together a narrative. This can "make us aware of our capacity for providing links" as well as our unique "preconceptions" (280).

While Asplund was certainly interested in developing individual self-awareness, it is less likely that he was completely dedicated to revealing an individual's peculiarities. His guiding impulse was to frame more general themes instead of concrete narratives. More specifically, he offers places dedicated to different ways

FIGURE 3.31 View of interior of Skandia Cinema, Asplund, 1922

Source: Swedish Center for Architecture and Design, ARKM.1962-101-0753

of thinking and experience. Stories may prompt those ways of thinking, but it is left to you to conjure them at will. For example, some visitors might ask if the dancing couple at the side of the water is Adam and Eve or Peleus and Thetis. Others might be content to conclude that it does not matter and proceed to enjoy the sparkling water and the view of others sharing this pleasure. The broader intention on Asplund's part is to display a geography of the emotions and suggest that each part—mountain, stream, reflecting pool, and library—is the dwelling place of different stories *and* different ways of thinking.

By virtue of the views and flowing water that connect different parts, he also wishes to quietly remind us that these different parts should not exist autonomously. While sitting on a bench alone on top of Observatoriekullen, for example, you might gaze at the wide panorama of the city with some Zarathustra-like sense of mastery. At the same, time, however, the reflecting pool and the dancing figures are never out of sight. As previously mentioned, late in his design process, Asplund attempted to develop a cascading chute of water from the hilltop plaza to the pool below. The stream and grotto carry out this idea, while allowing the visitor to imagine the true source of the water. The implied lesson of this connection might be that sensual pleasures and abstract thinking should never stray too far apart.

This union of sensual pleasure and more profound thinking is reflected in Asplund's response to the Greek temples of Southern Italy as a young man. One of his favorites was the Temple of Concord at Agrigento (Figure 3.32). His description reveals his acute sensitivity to both the ephemeral charms of the site and the more profound intentions of the builders:

> We have set out for the ancient Greek temples with awe in our souls. The road and the rocks a burning yellow, almond trees studded with white and pink flowers hanging over the stone walls, throwing off their lovely perfume and bearing thousands of buds. The grass strewn with flowers—white, red and yellow. . . . And then we came to the Concordia Temple, which has all its pillars and tympanums in good preservation—Gradually one begins to feel the greatness of this art. It is mighty and fascinating. We walked in the colonnades. To the north, between the time worn columns, we could see the town gleaming across the deep valley smothered in many-flowered almond trees. To the south, below the steep cliffs, the ground slopes irregularly down to the deep blue sea, on which a good fifty white-sailed boats may be seen far out sailing in line like a fleet on a warlike expedition. A wonderful spot, chosen with an infinite sense of feeling. A temple calls for height, the effort of the climb up to it induces respect. The high stair-like base enhances the impression as one toils upwards. And the great grave rhythm of the colonnade, rising in heathen grandeur before the Gods, as if simply rising before a higher and more harmonious being. . . . How beautiful it is to see a temple standing stationary in the verdure with trees around and no large sandy space in front.
>
> (Ahlberg 1950, 22)

FIGURE 3.32 Temple of Concord at Agrigento, Asplund, 1914
Source: Swedish Center for Architecture and Design, ARKM.1988-02-31

In this reconstruction of the intentions of those who chose this place and built the temple, there is the implication that they, like himself, saw this site on a beautiful spring day and felt the same sense of intoxication and grandeur. Though unstated, there is also the possible conclusion that the ecstatic experience of natural beauty and the appreciation of commonplace daily activities are the necessary companions to "awe in our souls" and approaching "a more harmonious being."

This analogy between inner life and landscape has much in common with Emerson's vision that the character of the world we see and remember is simultaneously the structure of our minds as well. Nature in these terms, he thought, is our original language. "Every appearance in nature," he writes, "corresponds to some state of mind, and that state of mind can only be described by presenting that natural appearance as its picture" (Emerson 1950, 15). For example, one might assume that the Stadsbibliotek represents a state of mind where all knowledge is envisioned. Following this logic, Wrede suggests that the rotunda is a metaphor for a human brain (Wrede 1980, 109). While this is a credible analogy, it is even more instructive, taking inspiration from Emerson, to claim that it is simultaneously a brain and a landscape. In other words, Asplund has used both landscape and architectural form as possible ways to imagine our consciousness.

While this analogy between inner experience and the outside world is certainly possible, there is also the potential to make more obvious parallels between the library and the outside world. This kind of calculated ambiguity, a well-known device of poets, is explained in Empson's *Seven Types of Ambiguity*. He would classify it as an ambiguity of the third type, "when an ornamental comparison is not merely using one thing to illustrate another, but is interested in two things at once and is making them illustrate one another mutually" (Empson 1966, 112). On a fundamental level, both library and hill have the status of prominent urban landmarks. On another level, the library intends to be a summary of the world—a panoramic view of literature and information. The hilltop, in turn, through the immediate juxtaposition of the library, presents the world as a library, however haphazard and disorderly.

It is fair to ask, however, how deliberate ambiguity, an appeal to individual discretion, might be related to a nationalist agenda. One answer is that this was one of the goals of the National Romantic painters. Prince Eugen's *The Forest*, for example, attempts to portray an archetypal dense pine forest with the glow of a sunset in the distance (see Figure 3.3). The sensation of an individual is bound together with a characteristic Swedish landscape; the awareness of self and national consciousness are made to be two simultaneous emotions. This was one of the intentions behind Asplund and Leverentz's initial design for the Woodland Cemetery, where heightened emotion was framed by a clearly identified Swedish landscape. At Observatorielunden, Asplund attempts again to translate this National Romantic idea about the identification of self and landscape, though in a less obvious way. While the simple ambient pleasures of shining water, sweeping views, and an accessible library are available to all, he offers ways to read all of these experiences together, prompting visitors to reach their own conclusions.

While this premise suggests an equal interest in the development of the individual and nationalist thinking, it is a very different agenda from others found in the West. Though the Stadsbibliotek was inspired by libraries in America, the ideology related to education or the development of the individual was far removed from Andrew Carnegie's gospel of wealth and self-improvement. Early socialist politicians were committed to education not so much for the realization of the potential of the individual as for a pathway towards more collective strength and dignity for the working class. Hjalmar Branting, in particular, spoke of individual freedom as "an illusion" in the face of coercion by capitalist power. He wrote of self-discipline and restraint on individual freedom as the only way to break this coercive power. The aim was to arrive at a new solidarity that would come with "the fall of privilege" (Tilton 1990, 27–28). This was part of a broader effort to remake Swedish culture and prepare it for socialist government. To make this happen, Branting put particular stress on *uppfostra*, meaning "cultural elevation" through self-education (23). ABF, the Swedish worker's educational association, and study groups sponsored by Kooperativa Förbundet were the primary vehicles for this cultural change.

Richard Bergh, the leading theorist among National Romantic painters, was sympathetic to the socialist cause but attempted to find space for individual creativity. Ellen Key was even more outspoken about the necessity of free creative expression, using Ibsen as the exemplar of uninhibited creative force (Key 1910). Bergh, however, wished to temper this imperative with a concern for solidarity. "Our individual freedom," he wrote, "together with feelings of solidarity, must create a new law and a new gospel. It will be the new day's work. Individual freedom [understood in the broadest sense] will no longer stand as a threat to feelings of solidarity" (Facos 1998, 114).

The problem of the individual and society also appears within the discourse of nineteenth-century Nordic authors and scholars who combined classical learning and folkloric interests. When explaining how there was a close identification with the culture of ancient Greece, Klinge observes that Gruntvig, a Danish clergyman, and others saw that Nordic people and the Greeks "were 'natural' people with their own mythology and folklore, as opposed to the more 'artificial' people, who did not create things themselves, but borrowed their culture from others" (Klinge 1986, 51). This sensibility is particularly well expressed in the work of Esaias Tegnér, a bishop and a professor of Greek. His most famous work is *Frithjof's Saga* of 1876, a work translated into multiple languages and known to all Swedes (Tegnér 1953). The hero must undergo all kinds of tragedies and tribulations before he learns to control his violent impulses and serve the greater good. After destroying a Viking temple, he flees to the Greek islands for a long exile. On his return, he reconstructs the temple with an open colonnade, following the Greek example, and resists taking revenge on his enemies. Through the agency of Greek culture, in other words, a heroic individual finds his true self through self-restraint and service to others. One possible message for Tegnér's audience was that the renewal of Nordic culture would come from an imagined union of Greek and Nordic traditions. Another was that it was possible for an individual to find an identity within a narrative of nationalism.

This concept of the ancient world is far afield from that which may be expressed by familiar Beaux Arts libraries in North America. Instead of rhetoric, philosophy, and science being at the service of self-advancement in a capitalist economy, Asplund, like the followers of Nietzsche and Nordic humanists, had in mind a legacy that is far closer to his experience at Agrigento, where gravity, sensuality, and the everyday come together. He communicates this experience not through a duality but through two parallel sequences of landscape and architecture. By virtue of the spatial context, however, there are multiple chances to reorder the reading and to make connections from part to part, or it can be enjoyed purely for its sensual qualities. When read attentively, the underlying purposes have much in common with the beliefs of National Romantic painters and Rutger Sernander. The emphasis, however, is on offering ways for the individual to reflect on more fundamental topics, which might include the inner life and the outside world, the purpose of a library, Nature and sensuality, and the well-balanced mind.

This kind of reflection could also serve a nationalist agenda. What is stunningly modern is that, without a coherent narrative, the individual is obliged to make a creative effort. Nationalism, or a sense of fellow feeling with others, is approached not through imposed values, familiar folktales, or a collective sense of superiority but simply through an opportunity to have an ambiguous experience related to knowledge, Nature, and sensuality. In Nietzsche's terms, the individual has a chance to "intensify the present" by sensing the meeting of fate and "chance and becoming." Asplund, in effect, provides his own answer to those struggling with individualism in a socialist society by inviting his fellow citizens to find their own path to common ground.

Notes

1 In correspondence with the author, Stuart Wrede notes that most of these figures are portrayed nude, including Queen Christina high up on the facade. He attributes this to the tendency on the part of the National Romantic and Vitalist painters to portray humans in wild nature in the nude, "stripped of all trappings of civilization."

2 See Arne Ruth, "The Second New Nation: The Mythology of Modern Sweden," *Daedalus* 113 (1984): 53–94. In the nineteenth and early twentieth centuries, many Swedish models of modernity were found in the United States. There were, however, long-standing Swedish traditions of fairness and egalitarian thinking. He notes the traditions of the eighteenth-century iron industry, where workers lived in factory villages called *bruk* and were provided with housing, medicine, and schools. There was also a tradition of rational administration in the public interest, going back to the time of Gustavus Adolphus. The memory of Engelbrekt Engelbrektsson, who led a peasant rebellion in the 1430s, was (and is) also very strong. Also see Christine Agius, *The Social Construction of Swedish Neutrality* (Manchester, UK: Manchester University Press, 2006). She explains how the consensualism of peasant culture influenced the governing of capitalist enterprises.

3 Asplund made a tour of libraries in 1920 with Fredrik Hjelmqvist to Europe and the United States. There was keen interest in the organisation of reading rooms in relation to book stacks and central circulation. See Hilda Lindstedt, "Några nyare Amerikanska biblioteksbyggnader med hänsyn särskilt till ekonomisering av utrymmet," *Byggmästaren 1923*, 290–92. They were particularly interested in Albert Kahn's library at the University of Michigan, where the main space of the library is on the second floor, surrounded by reading rooms. See Karin Winter, *Stockholm City Library: Architect Gunnar Asplund* (Stockholm, Sweden: Stockholm City Library, 1998).

4 It is worth noting that Piper's site plan for Drottningholm Palace Gardens indicates a spiral path to a small circular temple on a large mound that became the memorial to Gustav III (see Figure 1.2).

5 During the late twenties, the knoll at the North Entry of the Woodland Cemetery was under construction. Lewerentz, with Asplund's collaboration, had the responsibility for conceiving and detailing the Meditation Grove at this time. This particular grove at Observatorielunden, though possibly influenced by the work at the Woodland Cemetery, seems to have been designed for viewing rather than lingering.

6 This is the reminiscence of Åke Porne, an assistant in Asplund's office in the thirties.

7 This is a widely held interpretation that was shared with the author by Ewa Andersson, an administrator at the Stockholm City Library.

8 One of the leaders of this group was Oswald Spengler. It is ironic that Asplund drew heavily from Spengler's *Decline of the West* in the text of a lecture given in 1931, when he was appointed as a professor at the Royal Institute of Technology in Stockholm. See Gunnar Asplund, "Our Architectonic Concept of Space," *International Architect* 1, no. 8 (1982): 40–41.

9 This theory was shared by Ewa Andersson, a library administrator, in conversation with the author.

10 There is a drawing by Asplund that shows sculptures of Artemis and Actaeon, where the stream flows into the reflecting pool. See Engfors 1990, 27.

11 Ewa Andersson is an official at the Stadsbibliotek.

References

Ahlberg, Hakon. 1950. "Gunnar Asplund Architect." In *Gunnar Asplund Architect, 1885–1940*, edited by Gustav Holmdahl, Sven Lind, and Kjell Ödeen, 9–81. Stockholm, Sweden: A. B. Tibskriften Byggmästaren.

Andersson, Thorbjörn. 1993. "Erik Glimme and the Stockholm Park System." In *Modern Landscape Architecture: A Critical Review*, edited by Marc Treib, 114–33. Cambridge, MA: MIT Press.

Bergsten, Carl. 1923. "Stockholms Stadsbiblioteks Förläggning." *Byggmästaren 1923*: 305–8.

Constant, Caroline. 1989. "The Stockholm Public Library: Architecture between Nature and City." *Arquitectura* 280: 54–67.

Descola, Philippe. 2013. *Beyond Nature and Culture*. Chicago, IL: University of Chicago Press.

Emden, Christian J. 2004. "The Invention of Antiquity: Nietzsche on Classicism, Classicality, and the Classical Tradition." In *Nietzsche and Antiquity*, edited by Paul Bishop, 372–90. Rochester, NY: Camden House.

Emerson, Ralph Waldo. 1950. *The Selected Writings of Ralph Waldo Emerson*. New York: Modern Library.

Empson, William. 1966. *Seven Types of Ambiguity*. New York: New Directions Press.

Engfors, Christina, ed. 1990. *E. G. Asplund: Architect, Friend and Colleague*. Stockholm, Sweden: Arkitektur Förlag.

Eriksson, Eva. 2008. "Biblioteket och kullen." *Arkitektur* 3: 58–65.

Facos, Michelle. 1998. *Nationalism and the Nordic Imagination*. Berkeley, CA: University of California Press.

Iser, Wolfgang. 1974. *The Implied Reader*. Baltimore, MD: Johns Hopkins University Press.

Hamilton, John. 2004. "Ecce Philologus: Nietzsche and Pindar's Second Pythian Ode." In *Nietzsche and Antiquity*, edited by Paul Bishop, 54–69. Rochester, NY: Camden House.

Johanson, Klara. 1948. *Sigrid Fridman och Andra Konstnärer*. Stockholm, Sweden: Bokförlaget Natur och Kultur.

Jones, Peter Blundell. 2006. *Gunnar Asplund*. London: Phaidon Press.

Key, Ellen. 1910. *L'Individualisme (Images Idéales)*. Translated by Jacques de Coussange. Paris, France: Flammarion.

Klinge, Matti. 1986."The North, Nature and Poverty: Some Background on the Nordic Identity." In *Dreams of a Summer Night: Scandinavian Paintings at the Turn of the Century*, edited by Leena Ahtola-Moorhouse, Carl Tomas Edam, and Birgitta Schreiber, 48–53. London: Arts Council of Great Britain.

Östberg, Ragnar. 1929. *The Stockholm Town Hall*. Stockholm: P. A. Norstedt & Söner.

Porter, James. 2004. "Nietzsche, Homer, and the Classical Tradition." In *Nietzsche and Antiquity*, edited by James Bishop, 7–26. Rochester, NY: Camden House.

Sernander, Rutger. 1926. *Stockholms Natur*. Uppsala, Sweden: Almqvist & Wiksells Forläg.

Stern, Michael. 2007. "Pausing before Being: Nietzsche, Strindberg, and the Idea of Tragedy." In *Nietzsche and the Rebirth of the Tragic*, edited by Mary Ann Frese Witt, 40–71. Teaneck, NJ: Fairleigh Dickinson University Press.

Tegnér, Esaias. 1953. *Fridthjof's Saga*. Stockholm, Sweden: P. A. Norstedt & Söner.

Tilton, Tim. 1990. *The Political Theory of Swedish Social Democracy*. Oxford: Oxford University Press.

Wrede, Stuart. 1980. *The Architecture of Erik Gunnar Asplund*. Cambridge, MA: MIT Press.

4

THE STOCKHOLM EXHIBITION 1930

A moving landscape

Exhibitions in the late nineteenth and early twentieth centuries were used by organizers in a variety of ways. Some were designed to frame a nationalist statement about the host country, while others were more international in spirit.[1] As Bo Grandien has observed, because of the similarity of manufactured products from different countries, many exhibitors saw that the display of cultural artifacts and crafts was critical to commanding the attention of the public (Sandberg 2003, 187). What may have begun as a marketing strategy, according to Sandberg, set up a tension between a vision of progress and a longing to revisit traditional ways of life (187). Organizers, in other words, were simultaneously challenged to frame the future and to take a position about the uses and meaning of the past. With luck, visitors would come away with memories of a pleasurable experience as well as thoughts about the future and appreciation for vanishing handicrafts. Van Wesemael observes that organizers "saw the exhibitions as a means to make the individual conscious of his or her altering and globalizing experiential world, and thus to reconcile him or her with these changes by depicting them as evolutionary improvements of the old, trusted habitat" (Van Wesemael 2001, 21). Some, however, were not satisfied with these attempts and continued to pose questions about how to reconcile culture, the machine, and the quality of urban life for workers.[2]

In this context, the Stockholm Exhibition of 1930, designed by Asplund, presents an interesting case history. Here, Asplund and the organizers, who were supporters of the insurgent Social Democrats, were challenged to shape a Functionalist agenda to contrast dramatically with an earlier exhibition in 1897 on a nearby site. In addition, they also needed to respond creatively to the presence of Skansen, an open-air museum of rural dwellings across the lagoon (Figure 4.1) that had the status of a permanent exhibition. By virtue of this site for the exhibition, there was an opportunity to overcome the typical autonomy of exhibitions and form a more powerful argument about the quality of everyday life in past, present, and future. In this instance, landscape did not function simply as a pretty background for vast exhibition halls; instead, it asserted its preeminence as the unifying idea that embraced forest, small pavilions, performance space, and shoreline. The underlying message was that landscape could endow Functionalism with a reassuring legitimacy as well as poetic resonance. The outcome for some was a successful resolution of the lingering conflict between culture and progress. Others may have noticed, thanks to Asplund's poetic gifts, that landscape was made to float, glide, and travel by ship.

The idea to make this case in a festive context belongs to Gregor Paulsson, the director of the Swedish Society of Arts and Crafts. He intended the Stockholm Exhibition of 1930 to be a showcase for *Funkis*, or Functionalism, the Swedish approach to modern design of household products and architecture. In particular, he and his associates had two aims. One was to make a case against bourgeois living as a model for the urban existence of the masses. The other was to discourage rural nostalgia as an inspiration for design. For apologists of Functionalism, each of these rhetorical arguments has its nuances. On the one hand, bourgeois products were portrayed as continental, inefficient, and dishonest in their manufacture (Paulsson 2008, 79). The Swedish vernacular, embodied at Skansen, presented a more difficult case. Although rural vernacular had little to do with modern urban life, it reflected the collective life of ordinary people, an important theme of socialist doctrine. It also revealed an honest relationship between function, climate, and economy. Even more important was that it demonstrated a deference towards landscape as a primary organizing idea. By giving these rhetorical arguments visual form, the exhibition organizers attempted to resolve the awkward coexistence between traditional culture and the machine and offer a new understanding of the possibilities of everyday life.

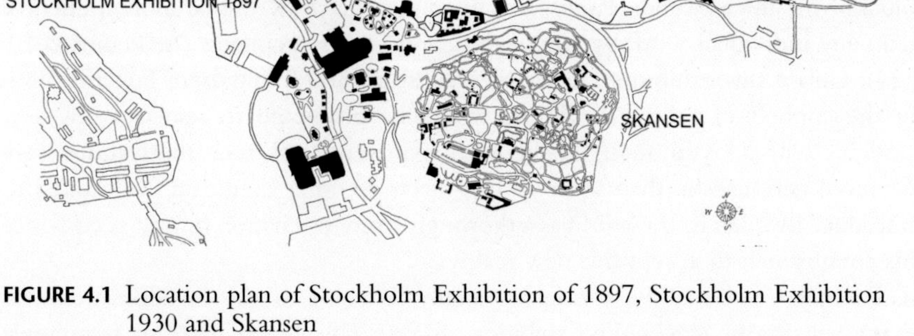

FIGURE 4.1 Location plan of Stockholm Exhibition of 1897, Stockholm Exhibition 1930 and Skansen

Source: Author drawing

This effort at resolution was not unusual in a country where compromise and consensus were the guiding principles of political life. In addition, because of a doctrine of neutrality, the country had avoided foreign entanglements in the nineteenth century and any involvement in the First World War. Comparative stability was the result, free of the financial and emotional toll of warfare. There was a compelling problem, however, related to housing. Because Sweden industrialized relatively late, there was a massive movement of rural residents to the cities after 1900. By European standards, Swedish housing was poor and expensive. Urban workers generally lived in appalling conditions, with families sharing two rooms (Rudberg 1998b, 17). In other words, the existing housing market helped very few to enjoy everyday life. Those who were dissatisfied with housing as well as limited opportunities in rural areas generally had only one option: emigration to the New World.

This was the great galvanizing issue that pushed those on the left and right to form a consensus. Between 1907 and 1913 the Commission on Emigration researched causes and solutions of the problem. Testimony about difficult conditions and aristocratic contempt was taken from immigrants in the United States and Canada. In this instance, policy-makers achieved a compelling vision of the negative reality of the everyday life of common people. This allowed conservatives and liberals to agree that government had to offer opportunities and a promise of a better life or risk a future of decline (Barton 1994, 147–65). This consensus did not result in comprehensive change, however, until the Social Democrats came to power in 1932, when their leader, Pier Albin Hanson, made an alliance with the Farmer's Party. Their slogan, *Folkhemmet* (a home for everyone), was both symbolic and literal. The party genuinely aimed to be inclusive, and its fundamental issue was housing.

The timing was opportune for Gregor Paulsson. On the one hand, politicians were motivated to support an image of progress and economic development. On the other, architects on the Continent were creating new designs intended to address the problems of a new era. Both Paulsson and Swedish progressive architects visited exhibitions in Europe and interviewed colleagues in the late 1920s who attempted to express this new movement. One important exhibition was the Weissenhofsiedlung in Frankfurt, where progressive architects built apartment blocks with efficient units. Paulsson claimed that this show was far more influential than any individual work by any of the contributing architects (Arrhenius 2010, 134). Unlike this exhibition, however, Paulsson wanted to present Functionalism in the context of a festival; visitors would be prompted to associate this new aesthetic with a joyful, though ephemeral, experience. Also, his motivations were far more nationalistic than those of organizers in other countries; he wanted to introduce Sweden to the world as a thoroughly modern nation as well as convince his countrymen to accept this new reality.

Paulsson's nationalistic mission naturally led him to use Swedish architects exclusively for the Stockholm Exhibition of 1930. The chief of his team, responsible for the site plan and most of the major buildings, was Asplund, the most celebrated

Swedish architect of his time. Though his previous designs were more characteristic of the Neoclassical movement, he was thoughtful about relating a building to the outdoors, both actively and symbolically. Asplund was also careful in relating meanings directly to function. At the Woodland Chapel, for example, the bereaved sit in a circle to comfort each other directly. At the same time, the circle becomes a cosmic dome overhead as a reflection of the heavens. At the Stockholm Public Library, a large rotunda makes a collection of books visually accessible and also offers an image of the Cosmos. Invariably, the inside of a building was conceived as a poetic meditation on the outdoors.

Asplund's talent in bringing life and meaning to buildings reflected the mission of the Society of Arts and Crafts in the decorative arts. They were dedicated to bringing artists together with industry to develop useful and beautiful household products for the masses. The idea for the exhibition was first proposed in 1927 by Gregor Paulsson, and it was immediately supported by both the state and the City of Stockholm (Rudberg 1998b, 35). "It was decided that the Exhibition should consist of three main sections: *household goods* likely to personalize a home, the *home itself*, its layout and design, and the *extra domestic urban framework*—viz. public transport and street and garden equipment" (36). It is noteworthy that not all board members for the society were completely in agreement. Suspicion of the machine and concern about the future of handicrafts were still widespread. As a diplomatic compromise, the mission statement for the exhibition was phrased to include both mass-produced items and handicrafts.

Despite this discord, there was consensus on the appropriateness of the site for the 1930 exhibition along the north shore of the Djurgårdbrunnsviken, a lagoon to the east of the city's center that was convenient to public transportation, with wonderful views and southern exposure (Figure 4.2). Across the lagoon is the site of Skansen, an open-air museum of Swedish rural life as well as the site of the Stockholm Exhibition of 1897 (see Figure 4.1). All three of these sites fit Foucault's description of the heterotopia as "other" spaces, removed from everyday life.[3] One of the functions of the heterotopia is to be the portal to an imagined place or utopia. Foucault speaks of this as a mirror where "I see myself there where I am not, in an unreal, virtual space that opens up behind the surface; I am over there, there where I am not, a sort of shadow that gives my own visibility to myself, that enables me to see myself there where I am absent: such is the utopia of the mirror" (Foucault 2001, 1575). Each exhibition site, however, offered a different version of the mirror that allowed instructive comparison with the others. Whereas Skansen clearly served as a portal to the past, the Stockholm Exhibition of 1930 served the same purpose for the future. In this case, however, the future is not portrayed as a world completely apart; rather, it sustains and enhances the well-known bond with the natural world. In this way, any sensation of loss of the familiar was to be compensated by a reintroduction to the well-being that derives from landscape.

Though it took place on the doorstep of Skansen, the Stockholm Exhibition of 1897 appears to have had very different intentions. Although one of its purposes in 1897 was to present the wonders of modern technology, many buildings were centric, with breathtaking interior spaces, suggesting an Ottoman influence (Figure 4.3). Each aspired to be its own version of the Cosmos, its own small church dedicated to a particular craft. As in other exhibitions in the nineteenth century, the design of landscapes and buildings was relatively autonomous and was not engaged in any understanding or interpretation of the products assembled. Instead, history was mined for an aura of wonder and intrigue that could exist quite independently of the actual exhibits. Pred asserts,

> Here, in terms of those who directly experienced it, was "a fantasy city," "a summer fairy-tale," "a toy city," "a dazzling painting," a sparkling jewel from *A Thousand and One Nights*. Here was a landscape whose Disneyland-like architectural rhetoric displaced the popular clamor for political (voting-right) freedom with images regarding the freedom to consume.
>
> (Pred 1995, 4)

The disconnect between form and content was even more egregious in a section of the exhibition called Gamla Stockholm, situated on its own island (Figure 4.4). Here a temporary town of one-half-scale historic buildings, most from other Swedish cities, was built in wood and plaster (Pred 1995, 69). In a deliberate effort to contrast with this historically inspired context, some of the buildings housed early examples of visual technology, such as displays of X-rays, projected slides, and early cinema. Though crowds were charmed by the illusion of time travel, many were alarmed when costumed soldiers would stage a daily fight in the town square. Again, the theatricality of the context tended to distract the visitor from the extraordinary qualities of some of the inventions within the buildings.

Because most displays at the Exhibition of 1897 tended to be dwarfed in cavernous buildings, space did not function in a way that permitted the visitor to effectively contemplate or understand products or technology (Figure 4.5). Advertising, meanwhile, had no visible presence in any photographs. Finally, the plan of the exhibition, besides the evocation of Old Stockholm, had nothing that would resemble the coherence of familiar urbanism. Large and small buildings were loosely arranged around a collection of roughly defined public spaces with little hierarchy or transition. A prescription for everyday life in this context can only be seen as the search for the extraordinary, either through sublime spaces or imaginary time travel.

Though Skansen may have imaginary time travel in common with the Exhibition of 1897, the agenda was very different. Sited on a hill in the Djurgården district to the southwest of the exhibition site, it was established in 1891 by Artur Hazelius, the founder of the adjacent Nordic Museum. Like many others, he recognized that Swedish rural life was disappearing and that without prompt action many of its most significant artifacts would disappear. As a result, threatened farm buildings from all parts of Sweden were reconstructed in a labyrinthine

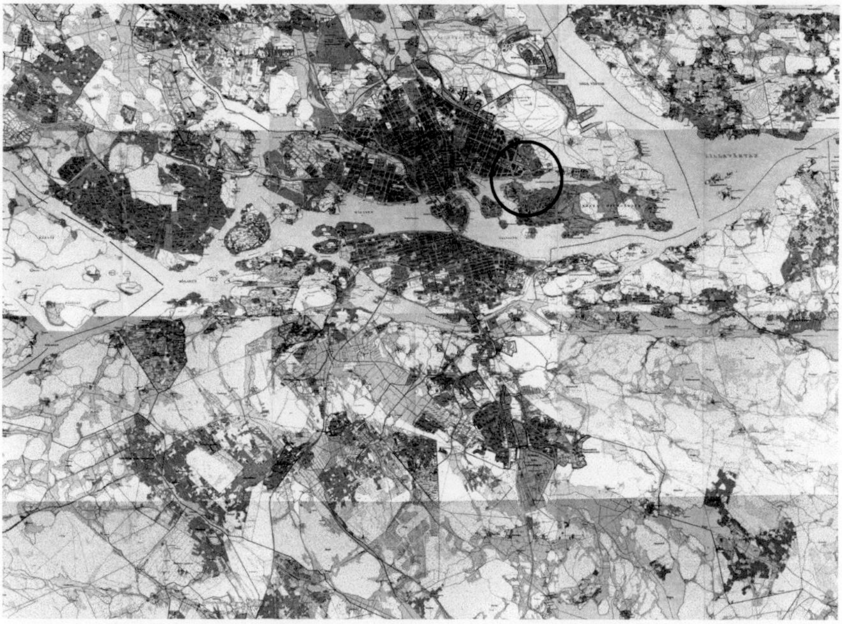

FIGURE 4.2 Map of Stockholm in 1934 with location of exhibitions

Source: H. Hellberg and A. E. Påhlman, Stockholm City Archive

FIGURE 4.3 View of Hall of Industry at Stockholm Exhibition of 1897

Source: Detroit Publishing Co., Library of Congress Collection

FIGURE 4.4 Gamla Stockholm at Stockholm Exhibition of 1897

Source: John Hertzberg photo, Tekniska Museet/National Museum of Science and Technology, TEKA0141965

FIGURE 4.5 Hall of Industry, Stockholm Exhibition of 1897

Source: Oscar Halldin photo, Tekniska Museet/National Museum of Science and Technology, TEKA0141979

suburban plan meant to create autonomous experiences without any coherent urbanism (Arrhenius 2010, 138) (see Figure 4.1). Great care was taken to reconstruct houses and outbuildings just as they were on their original sites, even to the point of importing soil and plants. Visitors could come into direct contact with spaces, clothes, and tools very much like those used by parents and grandparents. "The great thing about Hazelius's new museum," writes Rentzhog, "was that he collected items to do with ordinary people, the cultural development from the nobility to the very poor" (2007, 4). Though retrospective in his scope, Hazelius foretells the inclusive politics of Pier Albin Hanson's *Folkhemmet* by explaining how both rich *and* poor people lived in the past. This approach to public education was an astonishing success; after two years, Skansen was admitting five hundred thousand people per year. Given that Stockholm's inhabitants numbered only three hundred thousand in 1900, Skansen was reaching a wide segment of the Swedish population.

Though the locations at Skansen are not authentic, they reminded the Swedish visitor of family farms of recent memory. The intention on the part of Hazelius, for the most part, was antiquarian.[4] This kind of history, writes Nietzsche, "belongs to the preserving and revering soul—to him who with loyalty and love looks back on his origins; through this reverence he, as it were, gives thanks for his existence" (Nietzsche 1980, 19). This was done through the direct experience of interior and exterior spaces, both appointed with authentic furniture and artifacts. Within the antiquarian sensibility, however, lies the potential for other insights. It is worth remembering that many of the visitors in the thirties were not far removed from real experience in similar interiors. Certainly, on the surface, Skansen can be read as a nationalist expression of innate Swedish values. At the same time, it also has the capacity to promote other forms of awareness. For example, concerns about social inequality and suffering associated with rural life were common at the time. Just as the Commission on Emigration found an impetus to reform in their research, it is possible that visitors responded to physical portrayals of rural life in the same way. Any contemplation of everyday life, according to Kaplan, is by its very nature political. "Everyday life harbors the texture of social change; to perceive it at all is to recognize the necessity of its conscious transformation" (Kaplan and Ross 1987, 4). In other words, a retrospective view of daily life, staged within a museum, could have been effective at prompting critical reflection on the quality of the present.

Another source of insight could derive from a demonstration of fundamental principles of dwelling (Heidegger 1971), embodied in Swedish vernacular design. One of the first houses installed at Skansen in the 1890s was Morastugan, a log farmhouse from Mora district in the Dalarna region. This small cottage has a vestibule, one large room used for living, dining, and cooking, and a small bedroom. The large room also has box beds for sleeping, analogous to a Pullman car. The house was heated by a large chimney mass with multiple hearths. Significant improvements were made in the understanding of this farm when earlier outbuildings from the same region were added in the late twenties to form a fenced court with multiple entries from different fields and animal pens (Figure 4.6). Although the buildings were artistically related to the site by the architect Erik Lundberg, the site plan was based on the traditional configuration of Swedish farmsteads (Figure 4.7). The architect was so eager to compensate for lapses in authenticity that he gathered turf from the Mora region to be planted in the yard and environs (Arrhenius 2010, 143).

This farmstead, now known as Moragården, was reopened in June 1930, a month after the opening of the Stockholm Exhibition. During the period of the exhibition, the visitor count at Skansen exceeded 1 million for the first time and continued to increase. Because of its novelty, Moragården was clearly an important attraction at the time. It not only reflected the life of a less prosperous farmer, it portrayed some of the lessons that the exhibition organizers were trying to impart. As Ellen Key observed, the built-in features of Morastugan were "all fitting for their purpose, durable, and tasteful; nothing unnecessary and nothing wasted" (Arrhenius 2010, 140).

Whereas the spatial lessons of Skansen reside in small domestic compositions, the Stockholm Exhibition of 1930 captures them in a different context. Unlike the exhibition halls of the Exhibition of 1897, which were disconnected, those of 1930 were connected in articulated ranges of buildings, all with delicate colonnades (Figure 4.8). Though these buildings had relatively modest spaces, in contrast to those of 1897, they were meant to serve a larger agenda, whether advertising, daylighting, the display of enormous objects, or simply providing an observation platform for the crowd. Individually, all of these pleasures are commonplace and everyday. Taken simultaneously, however, with bright colors and flapping flags, the experience was electrifying for many. This association between objects, buildings, gardens, people, sunlight, wind, advertising, and color was used to create an environment of desire.

Though Asplund's intent was to demonstrate the potential of Functionalism, one source of inspiration may have been ancient. The pattern of exhibition halls on the Corso (Figure 4.9) is analogous to the closely packed temples and public buildings, some with upper galleries, on the Forum in Pompeii, a site visited by Asplund in his youth (Figure 4.10). Each pavilion simultaneously relates to the next as well as the wider open space. In the case of the Stockholm Exhibition, this forum was an open-sided space with a wide exposure to the narrow lagoon (see Figure 4.8). Within it were two "villages" of smaller pavilions within a dense grove of trees, as well as a terraced open space called the Festplats for large public performances. To the east of the Festplats, visitors could explore the housing area, a simulated street of model homes. Beyond this area, hidden from the major public areas, two amusement park courts were sited for those seeking more familiar festival pleasures. It is important to add that before approaching the housing area, a visitor had the option to cross a bridge over a narrow part of the Djurgårds-brunnsviken to visit the Bridge Coffee House and some smaller displays related to

FIGURE 4.6 Moragården perspective, Skansen

Source: Karl Gotthard Gustafsson drawing, *Trettiotalets Skansen*, Bokforläg Aktiebolaget Thule, 1939, Nordic Museum

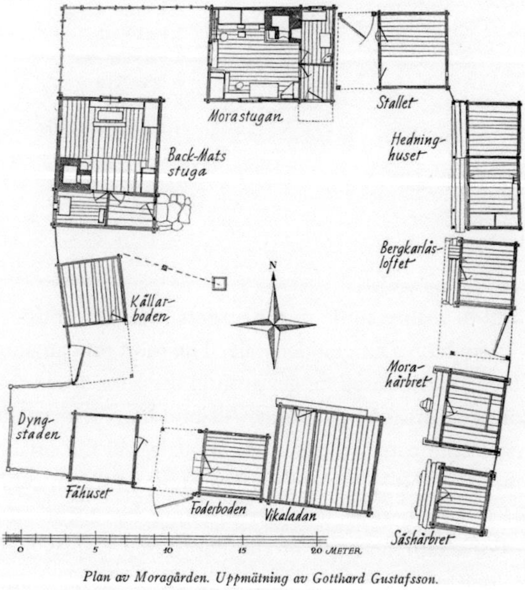

FIGURE 4.7 Moragården plan, Skansen

Source: Karl Gotthard Gustafsson drawing, *Trettiotalets Skansen*, Bokforläg Aktiebolaget Thule, 1939, Nordic Museum

camping, tombstones, and humorists (see Figure 4.8). Because this route also led to an exit that connected directly to Skansen, it can be understood as an attempt to engage the open-air museum as an extension of the exhibition. With the exception of the amusement areas, all spaces were oriented towards the light and the major public outdoor spaces. As a tightly choreographed spatial sequence, the idea for the Exhibition of 1930 lies in the complete urban composition, rather than a collection of breathtaking buildings, as was characteristic of the Exhibition of 1897.

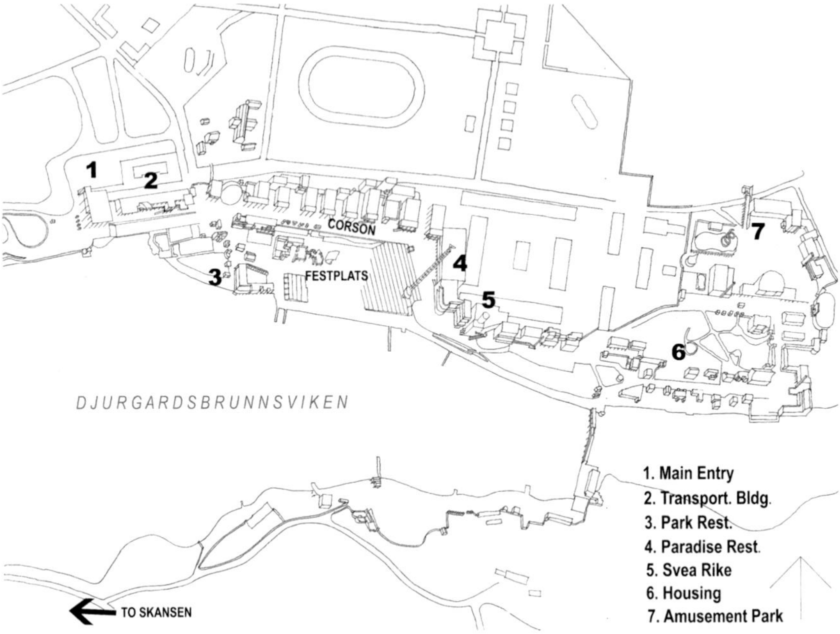

FIGURE 4.8 Stockholm Exhibition 1930 plan

Source: Author drawing after Ustallningenforläget

This strategy allowed Asplund to realize some of the essential characteristics of dwelling portrayed at Skansen, though on a far grander scale. The most fundamental decision was to wrap all buildings in articulated ranges around the large space that includes the Festplats and a forest with small pavilions. All buildings within this primary part of the exhibition are connected to this space. Equally, all the smaller subcourts and balconies are bound to this space as well (see Figure 4.8). In other words, spaces do not exist in isolation; they take on meaning by virtue of a connection to a larger place. For example, each of the connected display halls along the Corso, at the north edge of the Festplats, has a porch made of slender columns that, when seen as an urban composition, form a larger colonnade and serve as a spatial transition to the larger Festplats (see Figure 4.9).

What is particularly extraordinary is that despite the concern for relating spaces closely, the site plan does not rely on axial relationships between buildings or landscapes and buildings. This departs from the principles of classicism and the pattern set by all other major exhibitions in the nineteenth century, where large buildings were used as a dominating focal point and landscape was organized around the axis. This decision sent multiple messages. First, it declared that the meaning of the festival was *outside* and that buildings were intended to support that meaning. Second, symmetry, and all that it implies, was replaced by the need to accommodate particular circumstances, allowing flexibility to express the

FIGURE 4.9 Exhibition pavilions on the Corso, Stockholm Exhibition 1930, Asplund

Source: Gustaf Cronquist, The Swedish Center for Architecture and Design, ARKM.1990-106-027

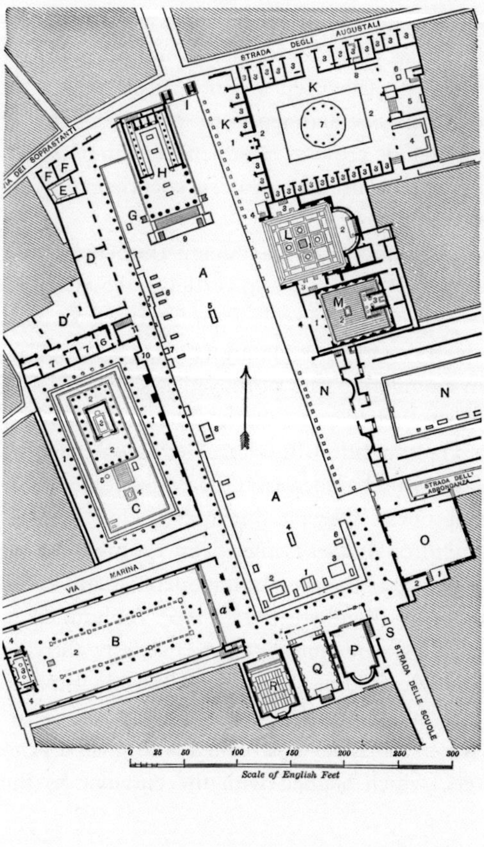

FIGURE 4.10
Plan of Forum, Pompeii

Source: August Mau, *Pompei: Its Life and Art*, London: Macmillan, 1907

function of a part without disturbing the order of the whole. In addition, although a major route was indicated, there was no axis that coerced the visitor towards one destination. Because of these decisions, landscape was no longer in a subordinate role, but enjoyed an equal status. Whereas previous exhibitions had placed the weight of attention on thrilling architectural experience, both inside and outside, Asplund shifted the emphasis to the experience of a place that included *both* landscape and buildings.

This intention implied a broader range of architectural expression that went beyond gathering spaces and making a location. Asplund's designs also propose that they can gather *things* into a relationship with buildings and landscape. In this case, he shows how signs, a forest, a flower garden, an airplane, and boats can extend the ways we see buildings and experience the wider world. First, this is reflected in the Transportation Building, located immediately beyond the Entry Building as the first building on the Corso (see Figure 4.8). This was a simple bar building with continuous open balconies which were interrupted by a series of articulated abstract pavilions. Each of these was dedicated to a certain kind of transportation: boats, trains, and airplanes. Instead of hiding the artifacts within, the architecture framed them for display on the outside. A hand-like structure embraced a racing yacht (Figure 4.11); an undulating roof complemented the hulls of small motorboats, and an airplane was suspended, seemingly ready for takeoff, from a shed-like form. On one level, he demonstrated that Functionalism had the capacity to display beautiful engineering as part of a façade, an unthinkable task for a Neoclassical design. On another, he associated a controversial style with engineered objects that had immediate interest and appeal to the public. In this way, while visitors enjoyed the sun, wind, crowds, a garden, and the lagoon, Functionalism was immediately connected with an enhanced experience of the world that one might have on a boat or a plane.

A critical part of this strategy of association was the Alnarp Garden, located immediately opposite the Transportation Building at a lower level, closer to the water.[5] The garden was named after a horticultural college in Southern Sweden and designed by Asplund in collaboration with Erik Bülow Hübe, a noteworthy landscape architect from Malmö.[6] In a rendering, it is portrayed as a very colorful flower garden where visitors would stroll as if in a gallery.[7] The main entrance was a staircase located opposite the Transportation Building. Before entering the garden, one passed a sculpture of entwined nudes by Carl Milles called *Two Dancers*, analogous to the *Youth* sculpture at Observatorielunden. Flowers were selected to ensure consistent blooming through the summer. Underground heating cables were used to bring tulips into bloom at the time of the opening, and lower areas were planted with water-loving plants (Rudberg 1998b, 106). A photo taken soon after the opening shows beds of tulips, while photos taken later show thriving annuals and perennials (Figure 4.12). Two winding stone paths allowed visitors to linger among flower beds just as they might in the rear plot behind a home. Immediately south of the Alnarp Garden, there was a path lined with small topiary figures, resembling birds and baskets, which aligned with the entrance to the

FIGURE 4.11 Transportation Building from Corso, Stockholm Exhibition 1930, Asplund

Source: C. G. Rosenberg Photo, The Swedish Center for Architecture and Design, ARKM.1994-112-2156

railroad display at the Transportation Building (Figure 4.13). While the topiary garden erased the distinction between plants and "things", the border garden can be seen as an appeal to domestic sensibilities and a reminder of the vitality of the natural world. Meanwhile, the architect also sought admiration for the boats and airplane immediately above. By these means, the Functionalist Transportation Building enjoyed the gift of association with beautiful engineering, the charms of a border garden, and curious boxwood figures.

Asplund attempted to conjure a similar spell at the Park Restaurant, located south of the Transportation Building, where a grove of trees met the water (Figure 4.14). Here, three idiosyncratic dining rooms surrounded a large kitchen that serviced all of them (Figure 4.15). One of these, called Puck, had a glass-vaulted roof with a pointed arch. It faced north, towards the forest, and allowed a view into the canopy of the trees. Another, located along the water, was called the Böljeblick, or "View of the Waves." It was articulated with small courts and niches to make space for the existing trees on the site. Finally, the most extraordinary was the Ellida dining room, located next to the Böljeblick, also on the water. It had an extremely light steel roof where three small trees came through the floor and emerged from the room. Meanwhile, the two floors of the Ellida were tapered in plan at the western end like the bow of a boat; the lowest floor appeared to float above the surface of the water (Figure 4.16). Ellida is the name of the hero's ship from *Frithjof's Saga*, the nineteenth-century epic poem by Esaias Tegnér. Bearing this in mind, it was possible to construct many different narratives about why a forest should be growing in a boat. Whereas the 1897 exhibition overwhelmed visitors with enormous spaces, here Asplund indulged in a gentle surrealism where the boundaries between things, trees, water, and buildings were blurred. In this case, it was implied that Functionalism could transcend the serviceable to arrive at a poetic union with the natural environment. More specifically, he demonstrated in literal terms that the phenomenal presence of the outdoors can persist inside. In addition, landscape was portrayed as if it were endowed with the capacity to move at will. For a people proud of their love of Nature, this was arguably the most potent possible demonstration of the new movement.

Another building designed to relate closely to the site was the Paradise Restaurant, a long building that enclosed the east end of the Festplats (Figure 4.17). Like the display pavilions on the Corso, the restaurant was located on the second floor, floating above shops on the ground floor and divided between a long section that faced the Festplats and a shorter one oriented towards the water. In both cases, the restaurants were terraced like a theatre, drawing the eye to the events on the Festplats and the active water sports in the lagoon (Figure 4.18). The terrace of the long section can be seen as a continuation of the terraced grade of the Festplats outside. In fact, Asplund originally conceived of this building as an open-air structure, like a grandstand with terraces of planters. Even though these patrons were more affluent, they were not isolated from the larger community. Again, unlike the introverted buildings of 1897, the rationale lay outside

FIGURE 4.12 Diagonal view of Alnarp Garden and Transportation Building, Stockholm Exhibition 1930, Asplund and Bülow-Hübe

Source: Gustaf Cronquist, Swedish Center for Architecture and Design, ARKM.1976-107-0494

FIGURE 4.13 Alnarp Garden, Stockholm Exhibition 1930, Asplund

Source: Florman and Halldin photo, The Swedish Center for Architecture and Design, ARKM.1976-107-2149

FIGURE 4.14 Park Restaurant, Stockholm Exhibition 1930, Asplund

Source: Källgrens ateljé photo, The Swedish Center for Architecture and Design, ARKM.1976-107-0528

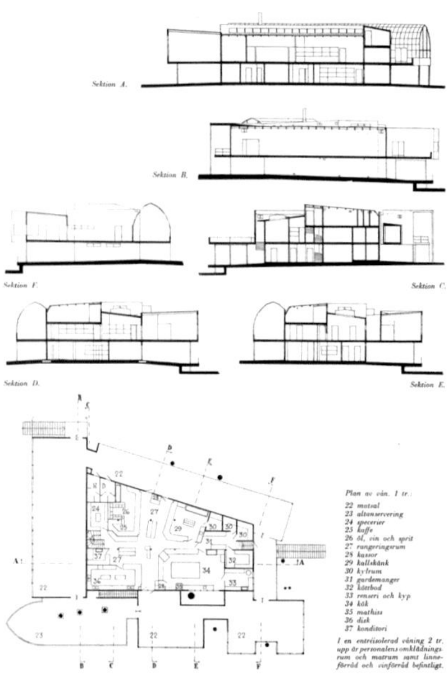

FIGURE 4.15
Park Restaurant plan and sections, Stockholm Exhibition 1930, Asplund

Source: National Library of Sweden, *Byggmästaren*, utställningensnumret 1930, 72 Ay Byggmästaren

FIGURE 4.16
"Ellida" at Park Restaurant, Stockholm Exhibition 1930, Asplund

Source: Källgrens ateljé photo, Svensk Form, SVF008742

in the larger idea of the exhibition. In this case, however, there was a reciprocal relationship between the observers and the observed; at night, a curved projecting bay housed dancing figures that could be seen from far across the Festplats. Also, this building and many others were illuminated at night with neon that cast a shimmering reflection on the lagoon from a distance (Figure 4.19).

A similar relationship between the observed and observer also existed in the Festplats below. Here, Asplund designed planting boxes on legs where the top of the box was roughly at table height (Figure 4.20). On a superficial level, these boxes of flowers served to animate a large space between performances. On another level, however, this concept served to place seated people within a garden, with their heads just above the plants. For those observing the Festplats from the Corso above, seated people with colorful clothes became part of the garden. From another perspective, those sitting within the garden were given a chance to closely examine the flowers in front of them while being obliged to accept them as part of the foreground of the performance. In this way, an idea of a garden is made to creatively coexist with a theatre, enhancing both programs. Finally, analogous to the Ellida, this portable garden on legs is a literal version of a moving landscape.[8]

This theatrical venue was marked in daytime and nighttime by the seventy-four meter advertising mast, located at the east end of the Festplats in front of the Paradise Restaurant (Figure 4.21). The traditional symbol of the midsummer festival in Sweden is the *majstäng* or maypole, some of which can be very large with numerous rings, stars, and crossbars. These represent the presiding divinities of the occasion. In an ironic twist, Asplund offered the advertising mast as a Functionalist version of the maypole, with logos of large corporations standing in for the symbols of ancient deities. At the top was the symbol of the exhibition, an abstraction of an Egyptian bird-man deity designed by Sigurd Lewerentz. To make it easier for those who might have missed the reference, it is worth remembering that the traditional version of the maypole at Skansen would have once been visible high on a hill across the Djurgårdsbrunnsvicken, next to the Moragården.

In addition to the cases already mentioned, there were smaller examples of thoughtful landscape design. Great care, for example, was taken to plant the reflecting pond along the edge of the Corso retaining wall with perennials and water-loving plants. Those flowers closer to a sculpture of a woman with a pot on her head, at the end of the pool, were planted in pots to create a transition between a landscape and a human figure (Figure 4.22). In another instance, smaller beds of flowers were planted in the courtyards of exhibition pavilions along the Corso. Because display areas tended to have continuous windows, many objects related to handicrafts and functional housewares were seen in the context of views of domestic flowers, the curving bandstand and people enjoying the lagoon (Figure 4.23). The strategy of visual association between landscapes, buildings and things could operate equally well at the other end of the spectrum.

The model house area was the second segment of the exhibition after the Corso and Festplats. It is possible to question this decision and argue that an

FIGURE 4.17 Paradise Restaurant, Stockholm Exhibition 1930, Asplund

Source: Gustaf Cronquist photo, The Swedish Center for Architecture and Design, ARKM. 1990-106-046

FIGURE 4.18 Paradise Restaurant interior, Stockholm Exhibition 1930, Asplund

Source: C. G. Rosenberg photo, The Swedish Center for Architecture and Design, ARKM. 1994-112-2168

FIGURE 4.19 Stockholm Exhibition 1930 at night, Asplund

Source: Gustaf Cronquist photo, Svensk Form, SVF004272

FIGURE 4.20 "Festplats" planters, Stockholm Exhibition 1930, Asplund

Source: Gustaf Cronquist, Swedish Design Center, ARKM.1990-106-173

FIGURE 4.21 "Festplats" with Advertising Mast and Paradise Restaurant beyond, Stockholm Exhibition 1930, Asplund

Source: The Swedish Center for Architecture and Design, ARKM.1976-107-0533

FIGURE 4.22 Reflecting pool garden with Corso pavilions beyond, Stockholm Exhibition 1930, Asplund

Source: C. G. Rosenberg photo, The Swedish Center for Architecture and Design, ARKM.1976-107-0535

FIGURE 4.23 Interior view from Corso pavilion with Orrefors crafts in foreground and garden beyond, Stockholm Exhibition 1930, Asplund

Source: Gustaf Cronquist photo, The Swedish Center for Architecture and Design, ARKM. 1990-106-069

exhibition about housing should have placed housing front and center. There is a logic, however, to Asplund's site plan. First, because the exhibition was to be presented as a festival or a celebration of collective life, establishing that context first makes sense. This imagined form of urbanism, where performances, commercial life, forests, and gardens coexist, makes the essential case for the quality of everyday life. Second, if the organizers intended to promote consumer desire for household objects, it was a convincing strategy to introduce the objects in a delightful public setting as an overture, followed by the objects in their appropriate domestic realm. It functioned, in effect, as a two-part sales pitch. As a prelude to visiting these homes, however, visitors were invited to visit a pavilion called Svea Rike, or the "Kingdom of Sweden," with many instructive displays about the history, economy, and folk life of Sweden. Films on traditional crafts made by Skansen were shown here. Paulsson and Asplund used this opportunity to make the case that the housing designs yet to be seen were perfectly in keeping with the progress of Swedish history and character.

Many different types of apartments and houses were built by different architects, all of them carefully tailored for people in different income groups. Small apartments for low-income families offered the greatest difficulties for architects. Kitchens had to be reduced to virtual closets, and daytime rooms had to function at night as bedrooms (Rudberg 1998b, 144–50). These apartments, however, did have bathrooms—a rare feature at the time. Among the many different types of houses displayed, the spatial qualities of the first part of the exhibition are best reflected in the terrace houses on display. Here, the direct relationship between sunlight, outdoor space, and indoor space is most apparent. One of the finest of these was Terrace House 45 by Uno Åhrén, featuring an open plan downstairs with a recessed outdoor terrace (Figure 4.24). This design anticipates a competition entry by the architect's office of the Cooperative Association in 1932, where an aerial rendering shows a Functionalist terrace house with a couple taking

FIGURE 4.24 Terrace House 45, Stockholm Exhibition 1930, Uno Åhrén

Source: Uno Åhrén photo, The Swedish Center for Architecture and Design, ARKM. 1985-109-300

their ease on the terrace and an elderly peasant tending to his vegetable garden among his fruit trees. The title, "One Day the Earth Shall Be Ours," makes the political intention obvious. Even more significant is that, like the Stockholm Exhibition itself, the work combines gardens, rural memory, the everyday, and Functionalist design.[9]

The linkage between rural culture and the new urban life was assisted by the modern curatorial methods pioneered at Skansen. Arrhenius has observed how the direct spatial experience of authentic interiors there was derived from the great exhibitions of the nineteenth century (Arrhenius 2010, 136). Hazelius, the founder of Skansen, turned this from a sales strategy into a pedagogical method. By virtue of bodily experience, according to Sandberg, visitors were invited to imagine "as if," temporarily planting themselves in the past (Sandburg 2003, 260). Paulsson and Asplund effectively adopt the same method, though repurposed for selling the idea of Functionalism. For those conditioned by the experience at Skansen, this borrowed method may have conferred legitimacy, making the future seem inevitable and equally Swedish. Yet the circumstances were unusual. Arrhenius explains that this display strategy

> opened up an ambiguity in that the "reality" of the exhibited model homes had to be communicated in a temporary framework, creating an intriguing interplay between a projected permanence relating to habitation—full scale houses presented as if they were lived in—and the exhibition's many ephemeral happenings—fireworks, water shows, fairgrounds—a combination that in part explains the "persuasiveness" of the exhibition.
>
> (Arrhenius 2010, 135)

This coexistence of the ephemeral and the routine is the latent irony of the Stockholm Exhibition of 1930. It is simultaneously about the everyday and a departure from the everyday. The 1897 exhibition, in contrast, offered literary spatial experiences suggesting time travel and the Ottoman Empire. These were clearly intended as an imaginative departure from the everyday. In this way, they offered a guide to experiencing the city as a potential dream world where architecture and infrastructure are portals for fantastic voyages of the imagination in the manner of Jules Verne or Victor Hugo. Walt Disney theme parks continue this tradition, inviting the visitor to participate in cinematic experiences.

The Exhibition of 1930, on the other hand, has more in common with Henri Lefebvre's description of the peasant festival.

> Certainly, right from the start, festivals contrasted violently with everyday life, but were not separate from it. They were like everyday life but more intense; and the moments of that life—the practical community, food, the relation with nature—in other words, work—were reunited, amplified, magnified in the festival.
>
> (Lefebvre 1991, 207)

Paulsson and Asplund did not intend the ecstasy of a harvest festival per se, but they did intend to make a commentary about desire and everyday life. The organization of the Stockholm Exhibition suggests that there are two kinds of everyday experience, public and private. Paulsson and his collaborators wanted to define the home, unlike the bourgeois home with its generous parlors for public reception, as a place of refuge, unburdened by the extra square feet required for entertaining. They used the Stockholm Exhibition to suggest that the greatest pleasures of everyday life lay in collective urban life and landscapes, outside of the home. Alvar Aalto, the celebrated Finnish architect, who attended the exhibition, wrote,

> One can understand the Exhibition has even aroused fierce criticism, being a surgical incision into the deep-rooted tendency to associate the concept of art with a genteel classy lifestyle and its exclusive artifacts. What this exhibition speaks for is a cheerful, uninhibited daily existence. It makes coherent propaganda for a healthy, unassuming way of living, based on economic realities.
>
> (Rudberg 1998b, 192)

If consumer culture might be considered to be the direction of desire, it can also be called the stuff of daydreams that make everyday life bearable. Paulsson and his collaborators attempted to use the exhibition to redirect desire so that Swedes would find satisfaction in *real* experience rather than objects or spaces that delivered fantasies. An object in the home, for example, should be desired for its capacity to be used every day rather than its reference to a spurious past. Likewise, the *real* experience of a city does not lie exclusively in the appreciation of magnificent buildings, historic or otherwise. Instead, it resides in the simultaneous experience of sunlight, crowds, signs, Nature, buildings, and machines. About the exhibition, Aalto explained,

> Here is no question of a composition in stone, glass and iron, as a visitor who despises "funkis" perhaps imagines, but a composition in houses, flags, floodlights, flowers, fireworks, happy people and clean table cloths. To Asplund a Finnish tourist who for one krona rides a waterbicycle on the Djurgården creek is a valuable object, bringing life to his exhibition. The surprising fireworks have the same right to be there as a showcase.
>
> (Rudberg 1998b, 192)

Because the exhibition was attended by more than 4 million people, this formula described by Aalto was an astonishing success. This is a remarkable statistic given that Sweden's population at the time was 6 million (Rudberg 1998b, 101).[10] Despite this popularity, immediately after the exhibition came down in October 1930, there was a backlash against Paulsson by a faction of the Society of Arts and Crafts led by a furniture designer named Carl Malmsten (197). They had many fears, chief among them the loss of national identity in arts and architecture, the crassness of overt consumerism, and the disappearance of handicrafts. These concerns were answered, soon after the exhibition, by several texts that were written to convince the disbelieving that Functionalism was in fact deeply Swedish, citing vernacular works and an innate preference for simple, functional things. The most famous among these is a polemical tract called *acceptera* published in 1931 by Paulsson, Åhrén, Asplund, Gahn, and Markelius, all of them involved with designing buildings for the exhibition. In contrast to the antiquarian approach at Skansen, this is a work of critical history in Nietzsche's terms. One who wants to make this kind of change, Nietzsche writes, "must have the strength, and use it from time to time, to shatter and dissolve something to enable him to live: this he achieves by dragging it to the bar of judgment, interrogating it meticulously and finally condemning it" (Nietzsche 1980, 21). He adds that those who engage in critical history are not immune from conflicts between "a strict new discipline and ancient education and breeding" (22). He explains that "it is an attempt, as it were, *a posteriori*, to give oneself a past from which one is descended—always a dangerous attempt because it is so difficult to find a limit in denying the past and because second natures are mostly feebler than the first" (22).

This kind of critical history requires a creative interpretation to elucidate a pedigree where none may have been visible previously. In this context, it is noteworthy that Paulsson had a doctorate in art history and the necessary skill to form different arguments presented in *acceptera*. In several instances, the writers present historic eras that date before the nineteenth century as models of cultural continuity. In these cases, dress, decorative arts, architecture, and even human movement were all of a piece. "In the past," they write, "culture was unified in character," and that unity should be the goal of the modern era (Åhrén et al. 2008, 290). They also explain that the gulf between architecture and the allied arts developed in the nineteenth century, when there was a widespread reaction against industrialism. The assumption at the time was that renewal would come from a revival of handicrafts as well as the patronage of the upper classes (241). "The romantic infatuation with farmer's cottages, antique furniture, and four-poster beds was a reaction to the cold, sober reality of industrialism" (290).

The authors of *acceptera* wished to present a united front to resist the forces that opposed Functionalism.[11] Most chapters make strident arguments about the need to accept the inevitability of Functionalism as a natural outgrowth of modernity, possibly inspired by Spengler's theories about consistency in all parts of culture in a given era.[12] Although regret is expressed about the decline of handicraft, the argument is made that only Functionalism and industrial production can deliver the greatest quality in housing to the greatest number of people. There are two chapters, however, that are distinctive in the relative nuance of arguments and a willingness to engage opposing opinions with the artifice of a dialogue.

These chapters are entitled "Old and New" and "A Chapter on Home Comforts." Though it is impossible to identify the author of these chapters with certainty, both touch on themes that are present in Asplund's landscapes and architecture and strongly suggest his authorship. One theme is a preference for the presence of different eras in our environment, an objective that Asplund had in most of his landscapes and buildings.[13] Another is a concern for tradition and "spiritual values." The author writes, "We do not want to be found guilty of defending a development at the expense of spiritual values" (Åhrén et al. 2008, 234). These values are not imparted by reproductions of farmhouses and furniture; memory, instead, comes from an owner's use over a long period.[14] Given Asplund's well-known preoccupation with the human body, another revealing passage compares the restrictions of traditional design to a corset; loosening the stays of this corset will be a stimulus to "imagination" to address the problems of the modern era. This supports Colin St. John Wilson's assessment that Asplund embraced Functionalism not so much to obey the imperative of new architectural programs as for its capacity to extend his architectural vocabulary and his range of expression (Wilson 1992).

Though the authors of *acceptera* were acutely aware of sociological change, their text does not reach a phenomenological understanding of dwelling as an expression of a collective sensibility and makes no clear statement about the role of landscape. While Asplund's design for the exhibition does reach this level, the authors of *acceptera* were not able to articulate the qualities of Asplund's design intuition. They did, however, succeed in framing a way of thinking about the modern era in contrast to other eras. Although it approached function in the practical sense, it also recognized the legitimacy of daily life and established an analytic discipline for understanding function more broadly in the future as dwelling.

In the succeeding decades, in fact, other Swedish architects had the chance to explore the implications of the lessons of *acceptera* and the exhibition. Although the spirit of a festival can quickly fade, as Lefebvre acknowledged, during this time architects did pose questions about the true nature of dwelling (Lefebvre 1987, 11). As Heidegger wrote, thinking is the first step in relieving the misery of the search in learning to dwell (1971, 161). Uno Åhrén, one of the authors of *acceptera*, took a decisive step in this direction when he explained how architects in the thirties erred in placing exclusive emphasis on the solar orientation of apartments, forgetting the importance of pleasure and communal life in public spaces—one of the lessons of the Stockholm Exhibition (Rudberg 1998a, 119). Once the scope of Functionalism embraced these factors as well, Swedish architects and planners arrived at a new standard for large housing developments. Examples include Rosta in Örebro by Backström and Reinius (1947–51), Baronbackarna in Örebro by Ekholm and White (1951) (Figure 4.25), and Nya Brukel in Sandviken by Erskine (1973–78) (122–23, 298, 338). All of these projects succeed in programming outdoor public spaces in a hierarchy of scale, preserving a direct contact with the landscape and compensating for modest spaces in apartments.

A large part of the success of Functionalism in Sweden can be credited to the power of the art historian as a cultural agent. Paulsson had the capacity to see how cultural unity existed in the past when objects and spaces reinforced each other. He was also shrewd enough to know that change which attempted to shape the

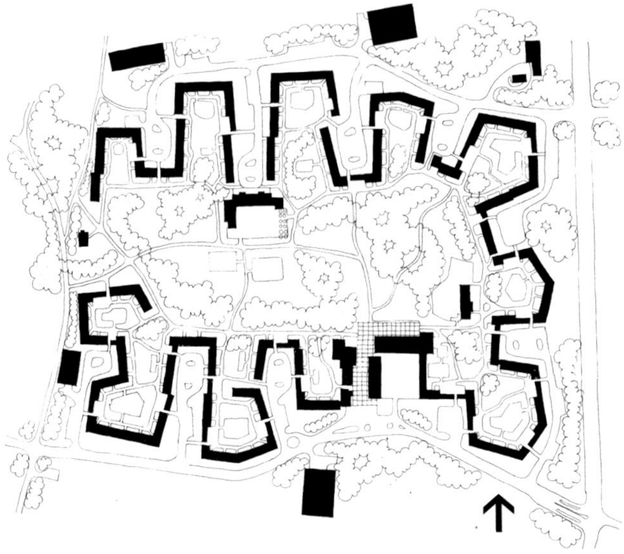

FIGURE 4.25 Baronbackarna Site Plan, Örebro, Ekholm and White, 1951

Source: Author drawing after G. E. Kidder Smith, *Sweden Builds*, 1957

taste of a new class of people required mass events on a par with the great exhibitions, not just books. He and his collaborators also recognized that associating Functionalism with trees, water, sunshine, Swedish flags, and gardens would give a positive visual form to both Functionalism and the progressive cause of the Social Democrats. In addition, unlike Germany of the thirties, where the vernacular was a propaganda vehicle for the Right, here the Swedish vernacular was used successfully to make the case for both socialism and Functionalism as an expression of a collective sensibility.

This was accomplished through the unique power of the exhibition as a place to imagine a different existence.[15] In this case, however, it did not exist autonomously, but actively used the memory and presence of Skansen and the Exhibition of 1897 as inspiration and foil. In this process, Paulsson and Asplund borrowed Hazelius's method of bodily experience of space to access the past as a means to introduce the future. Even more important, however, was Asplund's ability to frame landscape as the primary idea and to create a language for the expression of Functionalism *with* landscape. Though this form of design had traditional qualities, consistent with Swedish vernacular design, it was presented by Asplund at the exhibition as a phenomenon where sunshine, wind, water, trees, crowds, boats, and buildings became one experience. This message was quietly enhanced by Asplund's poetic devices, which allowed elements of landscape and horticulture to engage with a restaurant, an exhibition hall, and a performance space, all becoming moving landscapes of different kinds.

By virtue of these means that were both modern and traditional, they arrived at a vision of the future that was pleasurable, convincing, and meaningful. In effect, they used theatrical means of presenting the everyday which married dwelling in the phenomenological sense with dreams of a better future. This permitted the old schism between culture and progress, lingering from past exhibitions, to achieve some measure of resolution. It also established an idealized version of the everyday that would reemerge soon after when Asplund and Lewerentz completed the landscape for the North Entry of the Woodland Cemetery.

Notes

1 See John E. Findling, ed., *Historical Dictionary of World's Fairs and Expositions* (Westport, CT: Greenwood Press, 1990); Robert W. Rydell, John E. Findling, and Kimberley D. Pelle, *Fair America: World's Fairs in the United States* (Washington, DC: Smithsonian Institution, 2000); Cristina Della Coletta, *World's Fairs Italian Style: The Great Exhibitions in Turin and Their Narratives, 1860–1915* (Toronto, Canada: University of Toronto Press, 2006); Burton Benedict et al., *The Anthropology of World's Fairs: San Francisco's Panama Pacific International Exposition of 1915* (Berkeley, CA: Lowie Museum of Anthropology, 1983); Erik Mattie, *World's Fairs* (New York: Princeton Architectural Press, 1998); Paul Young, *Globalisation and the Great Exhibition: The Victorian New World Order* (Basingstoke, UK: Palgrave Macmillan, 2009); Matthew Rader, "International Exposition Sites in the United States, 1850–1975: National Historic Landmarks Survey Theme Study," n.d., on file at the U.S. National Parks Service.

2 Le Corbusier is noteworthy in this regard. He designed the Pavilion de L'Esprit Nouveau for the Paris Exposition des Arts Décoratifs in 1925. It was intended to demonstrate standardization, the capacity of reinforced concrete, and the potential for larger agglomerations of "villa-flats." Organizers did their best to conceal this project with a large fence that was later removed. See Le Corbusier, *Oeuvres Complètes*, vol. 2, ed. Alexander Tzonis (New York: Garland; Paris: Fondation Le Corbusier, 1983), 163–209.

3 This reference to Foucault is used as an analytic tool. Because the date of this writing is decades after the exhibition, it is not meant to suggest that this thought had any currency at the time.

4 Reference to Nietzsche in this context is not meant to suggest that Hazelius had any particular awareness of his works. Instead it is used to clarify different uses of the past.

5 Though the Alnarp garden is documented in photographs, no plan of the garden has been located at this point. As Eva Rudberg has observed, some portions of the garden survive. Through aerial photography, it may be possible to reconstruct a plan by discerning traces of the smaller pathways.

6 See Arne Wittstrand, *Stadens Landskap: Erik Bülow Hübe och Malmö* (Stockholm, Sweden: Carlsson Bokforläg, 2007).

7 Asplund was appealing to a widespread interest in all forms of gardening on the part of Swedes that had been promoted in earlier decades by Rudolf Abelin and Ester Claesson. See Catharina Nolin, *En Svensk Lustgårdenkonst: Lars Israel Wahlman som trädgårdsarkitekt* (Stockholm, Sweden: Bokförlaget Signum, 2008).

8 Asplund found many other opportunities to display flowering plants throughout the exhibition, including water-loving ones at the edge of a reflecting pool along the Corso and climbing plants at the edge of buildings. These are captured in color photos by Gustaf Cronquist in the collection of ArkDes.

9 This work is illustrated in Eva Rudberg, "Early Functionalism, 1930–40," in *Sweden: Twentieth Century Architecture*, ed. Claes Caldenby, Jöran Lindvall, and Wilfred Wang (Munich, Germany: Prestel, 1998), 80.

10 It is clear that many people visited on more than one occasion, thereby inflating this figure. The number of foreign visitors was estimated to be twenty-five thousand.

11 Creation for our times, the desire to be inspired by its brighter aspects, its dazzling technical inventions, its freer populace: this is all that can be meaningful. This interest, this endeavor to express the face of our age as its theme itself makes demands that we attempt to fulfill. We cannot be inspired by an age if we feel no loyalty to it. We must place ourselves at its service, we must help to solve its problems.

(Åhrén et al. 2008, 154)

12 Lucy Creagh mentions the influence of Spengler's *Decline of the West* on *acceptera* authors in her introduction to the English translation of *acceptera*. See Lucy Creagh, "An Introduction to *acceptera*," in *Modern Swedish Design: Three Founding Texts*, ed. Lucy Creagh, Helena Kåberg, and Barbara Miller Lane, 127–39 (New York: Museum of Modern Art, 2008). She also documents Asplund's borrowing from Spengler's concepts of space identified with different eras, outlined in *The Decline of the West*, in his inaugural lecture at KTH in 1931. These subjects are also treated in some detail by Eva Eriksson. See Eva Eriksson, *Den Moderna Staden Tar Form: Arkitektur och debatt 1910–1935* (Stockholm, Sweden: Ordfront, 2001).

Spengler also published *Art and Technics* in 1931, which expands on many of the themes from the earlier book. While it is understandable that Spengler's interest in the importance of origins and tragedy would have great interest for Asplund, he frames these themes very differently from Nietzsche. While Nietzsche and Strindberg are both inclined to think of the plight of the individual in the context of origins and culture, Spengler is focused exclusively on these themes in relation to conflict between races. Art for him is another aspect of weapon-and tool-making, and mankind is an inevitable victim of natural forces. Though this theoretical underpinning for National Socialism had its appeal in Sweden in the thirties, it runs contrary to Sweden's tradition of neutrality, its belief in itself as a model of progressive thinking, and its unique relationship with the natural world. Because it is not clear that Asplund ever abandoned these primary beliefs of Swedish civic life, Asplund's interest in Spengler should not be mistaken for an embrace of all aspects of Spengler's philosophy.

13 Culture suffers greatly if the progression of time does not appear naturally and clearly. The invigorating charm of cultural change is lost. The multiplicity of ages in our environment, with the genuinely old and the genuinely new, is valuable, adding richness to our lives in the same way as the differences between the ages of people themselves.

(Åhrén et al. 2008, 289)

14 Traditions and sentimental values are the feelings that bind us to the old familiar forms that we have seen since our childhood. Are they not something we should benefit from? For many this is certainly the case, but let us remember that we cannot through imitation endow what is new with the sentimental values of the old or the mood it inspires. These values are not created by architects, engineers or artists; we ourselves and time create them through the memories we attach to objects we have surrounded ourselves with during our lives and which have gradually become part of us.

(Åhrén et al. 2008, 244)

15 This could be understood as a heterotopia, Foucault's idea of a portal to an imagined place, expressed in "Les Espaces autres" (Foucault 2001).

References

Åhrén, Uno Gunnar Asplund, Wolter Gahn, Sven Markelius, Gregor Paulsson, and Eskil Sundahl. 2008. "Acceptera." In *Modern Swedish Design: Three Founding Texts*, edited by Lucy Creagh, Helena Kåberg, and Barbara Miller Lane, 140–347. New York: Museum of Modern Art.

Arrhenius, Thordis. 2010. "The Vernacular on Display: Skansen Open-Air Museum in 1930s Stockholm." In *Swedish Modernism: Architecture, Consumption and the Welfare State*, edited by Helena Mattsson and Sven-Olov Wallenstein, 134–49. London: Black Dog.

Barton, H. Arnold. 1994. *A Folk Divided: Homeland Swedes and Swedish Americans, 1840–1940*. Carbondale, IL: Southern Illinois University Press.

Foucault, Michel. 2001. "Les Espaces autres." In *Dits et écrits*, edited by Daniel Defert and François Ewald, 1571–81. Paris, France: Gallimard.

Heidegger, Martin. 1971. "Building Dwelling Thinking." In *Poetry, Language, Thought*, 145–61. New York: Harper and Row.

Kaplan, Alice, and Kristin Ross. 1987. "Introduction." In "Everyday Life," edited by Alice Kaplan and Kristin Ross, special issue, *Yale French Studies*, no. 73: 1–4.

Lefebvre, Henri. 1987. "The Everyday and Everydayness." In Everyday Life," edited by Alice Kaplan and Kristin Ross, special issue, *Yale French Studies*, no. 73: 7–11.

——. 1991. *Critique of Everyday Life*. Vol. 1. Translated by John Moore. London: Verso.

Nietzsche, Friedrich. 1980. *On the Advantage and Disadvantage of History for Life*. Translated by Peter Preuss. Indianapolis, IN: Hackett.

Paulsson, Gregor. 2008. *Better Things for Everyday Life*. In *Modern Swedish Design: Three Founding Texts*, edited by Lucy Creagh, Helena Kåberg, and Barbara Millar Lane, 72–125. New York: Museum of Modern Art.

Pred, Allan. 1995. *Recognizing European Modernities: A Montage of the Present*. London: Routledge.

Renzhog, Sten. 2007. *Open Air Museums: The History and Future of a Visionary Idea*. Stockholm, Sweden: Jamtli Forläg and Carlsson BokForläg.

Rudberg, Eva. 1998a. "Building the Welfare of the Folkhemmmet 1940–60." In *Sweden: Twentieth Century Architecture*, edited by Claes Caldenby, Jöran Lindvall, and Wilfred Wang, 111–41. Munich, Germany: Prestel.

——. 1998b. *The Stockholm Exhibition 1930*. Stockholm, Sweden: Stockholmia Förlag.

Sandberg, Mark. 2003. *Living Pictures Missing Persons*. Princeton, NJ: Princeton University Press.

Van Wesemael, Pieter. 2001. *Architecture of Instruction and Delight*. Rotterdam: 010.

Wilson, Colin St. John. 1992. "Gunnar Asplund and the Dilemma of Classicism." In *Architectural Reflections: Studies in the Philosophy and Practice of Architecture*, 138–55. London: Butterworth Architecture.

5

THE WOODLAND CEMETERY PART II

A home for everyone

The history of the final stage of the Woodland Cemetery is by no means simple. On one hand, it is a story of triumph, where the design of the North Entry both delivered on the promise of the Tallum scheme through the primacy of landscape, while on the other, it also reflected the ethos of a developed socialist nation. This was done through an alchemy of ambiguity and consensus. The result continues themes from the Woodland Chapel, including the importance of the approach on foot and an architecture that resists monumentality. By these means, the bereaved have the capacity to perceive what they wish. At the same time, there is a will to use antiquity to serve modern needs, continuing the Nietzschean humanism of the Stadsbibliotek and Observatorielunden. Most of all, it reveals the capacity of landscape *with* architecture to give a monumental presence to an individual's loss, where isolation and community each play a role.

This success was not the work of Asplund exclusively. It was Lewerentz who had the responsibility for site design in the twenties and early thirties. Unlike most architectural projects, the idea for the site was established first. Both architects then took their turns to design an appropriate crematorium. The decisive plan was presented in 1924; in it, a knoll appears as the termination of the Way of the Seven Wells for the first time. Though it was initially to be cloaked in a forest, this knoll was the critical move that established a monumentality for the landscape and opened the door for the further development of the North Entry in the next decade. Despite the promise of this breakthrough, it took many years before the project regained momentum.

Initially a crematorium with a "dogtrot" passage was shown to the southeast of the knoll as the focal point for what became the Way of the Cross. According to Constant, this was originally shown as a Neoclassical design that was closely related to Lewerentz's Resurrection Chapel. Soon after, he elaborated upon this design with a Neoclassical complex of offices and services around the large exedra, a semi-circular plaza, at the entrance (Constant 1994, 80). Though the exedra was built, neither the Neoclassical chapel nor the entrance buildings were constructed. In the wake of these proposals, Lewerentz concentrated on the layout of roads and burial areas. Asplund, meanwhile, took responsibility for small design projects such as furnishings, benches, and drinking fountains (81).

The architects returned to the problem of the North Entry in 1930, when they were given the problem of placing a large sculpture by John Lundqvist called *Resurrection* with an obelisk. Because the Cemetery Board was not satisfied with their proposals, a committee of distinguished architects, including Ragnar Östberg, Sigurd Curman, and Lars Israel Wahlman, was appointed to advise about work at the North Entry. They had suggestions about removing all service buildings from the North Entry and moving the obelisk and sculpture to a location just beyond the exedra. They also expressed a consensus that the landscape beyond the exedra should be left open and free of graves (Constant 1994, 82). Though their proposals were not followed in every respect, these comments were decisive in inspiring the architects to achieve the clarity of the final design of the landscape. This is captured in an aerial photo from around 1934 which shows the large knoll, the site for the future crematorium and a looping approach for automobiles through a birch forest, yet to be planted (Figure 5.1).

Though the knoll at the Woodland Cemetery is extraordinary, it is worth mentioning that prehistoric mounds are a familiar part of the Swedish landscape. They were sited most frequently in terrain that did not lend itself to cultivation. Most villages in Central and South Sweden, in particular, have burial sites close by. "The medieval law books show a clear relationship between a person's right to own land and farm it and his ability to prove that he is related to 'those in the tumulus'" (Sporrong 2008, 147). The mound was also used in monumental contexts, the most famous example being Gamla Uppsala, the center of the Old Norse religion, located near the university town of Uppsala, north of Stockholm. This was the location of the celebrated Temple of Uppsala, described by Adam von Bremen as a large wooden structure with a gold chain around it. Just outside grew a large evergreen tree, thought to be the Swedish version of Yggdrasill, a famous tree in Norse cosmology. In addition, Adam records that there was a sacred well nearby, as well as a sacred grove of trees. According to him, both were involved in the sacrifice of human victims (Bremen 1959, 207–08).[1] Other features of the site include three large conical mounds that were thought at one time to be dedicated to the gods Thor, Odin, and Freyr but are also considered to be burial sites of three kings of the Ynglinga dynasty. A photo captures the three Royal Mounds and the church at Gamla Uppsala (1100–1200) in the background (Figure 5.2). There were once as many as 2,000–3,000 barrows in the area; only 250 remain today due to erasure by agriculture. Though relatively little is known about ancient religious rites, the site does confirm a traditional bond between death, religion, and landscape.

This tradition is also one of the inspirations for the work of Fredrik Magnus Piper and Gustav III at Drottningholm, a royal palace west of Stockholm, mentioned in the introduction. Here, Piper executed a memorial garden for King Gustav III between 1780 and 1810. This was located on a large parcel immediately north of the palace gardens (1680–1728) by Nicodemus Tessin the Younger, Baroque parterre gardens in the manner of Le Nôtre. Though the ground was very swampy, with a stream flowing through it, Piper, with the collaboration of the king, succeeded in making a landscape here that was inspired by English gardens, which he had studied in some detail.[1] He relied on focal points that are linked by multiple axes both within the new park and through the existing palace garden (see Figure 1.2) (Bauer 1981).

Besides the relative autonomy of the park, what is most noteworthy is the decision to give preeminence to a large mound and grove located on a simulated island defined by canals, serving to isolate the mound and give it a floating quality. This was later used to memorialize Gustav III after his assassination in 1792 (Figure 5.3). It is even more extraordinary that the memorial grove becomes a series of radiating lines of lime trees that make visual corridors to honor important axes (see Figure 1.2). Instead of marking a natural landscape with monumental significance with a stone edifice, Piper and the king constructed their own version of a monumental landscape in the tradition of the forebears who made Gamla Uppsala. They also added an overlay of abstraction in the form of the radiating lime trees. In this way, they presented an ambiguous formula that is simultaneously nationalist and international, archaic and contemporary, abstract and Picturesque.[2]

In many respects, Asplund and Lewerentz repeated the same ambiguous formula 150 years later in very different circumstances. Contrary to the relative openness of the garden at Drottningholm, the Woodland Cemetery has an unfolding procession that reveals the open landscape (Figure 5.4). It begins at Sockenvägen with a large semi-circular plaza, defined by a retaining wall (Figure 5.5). This space functions as a gathering area for large groups and leads to a narrow corridor, like the entry hall of a Roman house, that restricts the view to the cross at the top of the hill and part of the Monument Hall. At the end of this corridor the view opens dramatically to reveal the wide landscape with the Meditation Grove on top of the knoll (Figure 5.6). This is a point where the various possible routes diverge. Auto traffic can either go left or right for service and delivery of passengers. Pedestrians, meanwhile, can choose between a route that travels towards the Monument Hall at the edge of the columbaria on the left or straight ahead on the Way of the Cross, separated from the other path by a low wall with sculpted wych elms (*Ulmus glabra* "Camperdownii").

If one proceeds on the Way of the Cross, there are several places that draw the eye. The wych elms in the Meditation Grove are trimmed to form a cloud that floats above the profile of the knoll. Also, the knoll gently slopes towards the southeast with discernible lumps akin to the form of a body. One of these is the Hill of Repose, with catafalque and plaza for outdoor services. For those too aggrieved to look up, the limestone pavement pattern of the path, inspired by a street in Pompeii, provides a source of distraction (Figure 5.7). Though the Monument Hall disappears completely at the bottom of the hill, it comes into view

FIGURE 5.1
Aerial view at North Entry of Woodland Cemetery looking north, Lewerentz and Asplund, 1934

Source: The Swedish Center for Architecture and Design, ARKM. 1973-103-083-1129

FIGURE 5.2
View of Royal Mounds at Gamla Uppsala, fifth and sixth centuries AD

Source: Countymuseum of Uppsala, Upplandsmuseet, Up260

FIGURE 5.3
View of Gustav III Memorial, Drottningholm Palace Gardens, Fredrik Magnus Piper

Source: Author photo

FIGURE 5.4
Final Plan of the North Entry, Woodland Cemetery, Asplund, 1940

Source: Collection du Centre Canadien d'Architecture/ Canadian Center for Architecture, DR1984:1650

FIGURE 5.5 Exedra at North Entry, Woodland Cemetery, Asplund, 1924–40

Source: Author photo

FIGURE 5.6 View of Meditation Grove, Woodland Cemetery, Lewerentz and Asplund, 1933–40

Source: C. G. Rosenberg photo, The Swedish Center for Architecture and Design, ARKM.1962-101-0852

again as one passes the chapels on the left, with modest forecourts. The courtyards within are almost completely concealed from view, with the exception of a grove of trees that appears to grow out of the roof of the crematorium (Figure 5.8). This phenomenon brings to mind the forest growing in the Ellida Restaurant at the Stockholm Exhibition and shows Asplund's continuing interest in blurring boundaries between the outside to the inside. Just before one arrives at the Monument Hall, there is a beautiful clock that hangs from an elegant arm on the left. While this serves a literal purpose for those concerned about the time of a service, it also acts as a *memento mori* like the motto at the gateway of the Woodland Chapel, "Hodie mihi, gras tibi" (Figure 5.9).

Once you arrive at the Monument Hall, there is an opportunity to pause and survey the landscape anew. The columns of the grand compluvium, clad in stone, frame a view of the Meditation Grove with the Hill of Repose and a reflecting pool in the foreground (Figure 5.10). Thanks to large openings in the adjacent wall, a courtyard with a grove of trees is revealed around the corner, explaining the phenomenon of the trees growing through the roof (Figure 5.11). Meanwhile, Lundqvist's aforementioned sculpture *Resurrection* lies just below the opening in the compluvium (Figure 5.12). Finally, this is also an occasion to turn around and appreciate the view, looking down the hill to the entrance, of the Way of the Cross.

This sequence shows acute sensitivity for those with different needs and interests. Once the open landscape is revealed, with its two very different sides and possible routes, there are several possible responses. One can focus exclusively on small gestures like the clock and the texture of the pavement and the entrances to chapels or attempt to embrace *both* small gestures and the monumental landscape. This sense of accommodation even extends to spiritual affiliation. A Christian can find some consolation in the presence of the cross at the top of the hill. Meanwhile, a visitor without Christian beliefs can take some comfort in the dominance of the knoll and the Meditation Grove.

In the context of the larger political culture of Sweden at the time, this emphasis on choice might be said to reflect the thinking of Per Albin Hansson, the Social Democrat leader who invented the concept of *Folkhemmet*, which saw the Swedish state as a home for everyone. He was careful to explain that this was not to be understood as a paternalistic state where different people would be coerced to do what was good for them. Instead, he wanted it to be thought of as democratization, where citizens would be asked to contribute their opinions and capitalists would be prevented from taking advantage of the powerless. This form of rhetoric was very useful to keep a broad coalition together that included working people, the middle class, and farmers (Tilton 1990, 125–44). It was this coalition that brought the socialists to power in 1932 and sustained them through the thirties.

In practice, Swedish socialism was not as simple as its rhetoric might indicate. Unlike other models, it was not exclusively a top-down process where the state was the only actor. Instead, progressive change and reforms most often originated with the cooperative movement, a branch of union activity. The most

FIGURE 5.7 View of The Way of the Cross, Woodland Cemetery, Asplund, 1933–40

Source: Author photo

FIGURE 5.8 View of Woodland Crematorium chapels, Woodland Cemetery, Asplund, 1933–40

Source: Author photo

FIGURE 5.9 View of clock, Woodland Cemetery, Asplund, 1933–40

Source: Author photo

FIGURE 5.10 View of reflecting pool, Hill of Repose and Meditation Grove, Woodland Cemetery, Asplund, 1933–40

Source: Author photo

well-known cooperative institution was, and continues to be, Kooperativa Förbundet (the Cooperative Union). Founded in the early twentieth century, by the thirties it had intervened in countless monopolistic markets, including galoshes, light bulbs, flour, and many other items, by launching its own manufacturing facilities. Sometimes even the threat of a market intervention by KF restored fair pricing to a particular market. It is notable that KF was an early advocate of Functionalism, creating their own architectural office to design plants and employee housing (Childs 1947, 1–28).

Affordable housing was a more complex equation. This cooperative initiative was led by the Tenants Savings Bank and Building Society. It collaborated with the Stockholm Cooperative Union and the state to build both affordable and superior housing, again in the Functionalist style. Prospective tenants would make deposits at different levels that would be subsidized by state investment. The least affluent made no deposit and were completely subsidized. Though there were cases where social engineering was pushed to an extreme, particularly in the realms of hygiene and population control, socialism largely appeared in the guise of collective action of this kind without the curse of coercion (Childs 1947, 51–64).

Because housing was at the core of Social Democratic ideology, spending on housing became the primary way to stimulate the economy during the thirties (Childs 1947, 94). Low-rise public housing blocks were built in Stockholm and other urban areas, many of them bordering public parks. "A mid-nineteenth century interest in homes grew into cooperation between non-profit-making organizations, big industry and the central government; this favored the growth

FIGURE 5.11 View of poplar grove in court, Woodland Crematorium, Asplund, 1933–40

Source: Author photo

FIGURE 5.12 *Resurrection Monument*, sculpture at Monument Hall, John Lundqvist

Source: Author photo

of the home furnishing industry. Culminating in the 1950s, this long process uniquely combined research, ideology, practical knowledge, aesthetic ambitions and industrial production" (Wickham 1998, 199).

Homes, according to Wickham, were invested with the primary goals of Swedish culture, shaping children, fostering democratic values, and promoting beauty and high standards. This new consensus was not led by one visionary artist or architect. Instead, it was shaped by public officials, interest groups, scientists, poets, artists, and architects. It had a political dimension as well; they not only defined the desirable landscape and the beautiful home but went on to declare that every Swede had a right to enjoy them (125).

Because the Swedish urban home was invested with the national ambition to embrace modernity, memory had little presence here. Instead, in Stockholm, it was lodged in parks that preserved rugged and sweeping landscapes. A form of urbanism where modern housing blocks abut ragged, open spaces became an accepted approach for urban living. This pattern represents the union of the cult of the modern home with the memory of the rural landscape; everyday efficiency was bonded with an artifact of natural space once enjoyed by ancestors. Though these parks were places of amenity, they also spoke of natural cycles, decay, and loss of a way of life. In this way death had a latent presence in the everyday.

While relentless efficiency was quite obvious in the model homes section of the Stockholm Exhibition, this other agenda had its presence in the planning of the exhibition halls and the open landscape. Here, the lagoon and the Festplats were identified with pleasure and collective activity, while the perimeter was devoted to display and commerce. Housing, or the everyday life of families, however, was the underlying subtext. In other words, the site plan was a demonstration of an ideal relationship of housing to landscape. This was to be realized in countless projects in Sweden, exemplified by the famous photo of mothers and children at Fredhäll (1936–38) by K. W. Gullers (Figure 5.13).

At the North Entry of the Woodland Cemetery, this equation is reversed; here the open landscape is the domain of the individual while collective life, meaning memorial services, takes place on the edge. Just as an American cemetery of the mid-nineteenth century, such as Mount Auburn, foretold the advent of a suburban movement, the North Entry likewise appears to consecrate a pattern for housing. Though the chapels face west, as convention dictated, it is inescapable that the prospect from them onto the open landscape would be sought after by any Stockholm resident. In this way, a pattern of a desired place for an everyday urban existence becomes the dream of a permanent resting place.

However desirable, this view of a knoll in an open landscape is by no means typical of an urban place or a natural place. The knoll is accessed by slightly recessed staircases on the north and south sides. The Meditation Grove at the top of the knoll is a paved square, with benches surrounded by wych elms (*Ulmus glabra* "Horizontalis")[3] that allow a view of the horizon all around and a view of the sky above (Figure 5.14). From a distance the foliage of the elms floats like a cloud, allowing the profile of the knoll to read continuously. The slope of the

FIGURE 5.13 Park at Fredhäll, Osvald Almqvist, early thirties

Source: K. W. Gullers photo, Nordic Museum, NMA.0033916

knoll is relatively steep on the north side, while it is far more gradual to the south. Clearly it is intended to be viewed from the north, east, and south because the western side is steeply graded to allow the passage of a service road in the area of a former gravel pit.

As a high place, this is equivalent to the small observation plaza at Observatorielunden and the top of the outcrop at Stennäs. It is ironic that a quiet place of individual reflection would be the focus of a vast public space. The emphasis, in other words, is not on the chapel, a place for collective commemoration, but on the very personal ordeal of the individual. It is also worth remembering that unlike its counterparts at Observatorielunden and Stennäs, this is not a natural place. It does not have the authenticity of the pine forest immediately adjacent. Instead, it is an obviously designed landscape that simulates the qualities of a natural high place. In this way, it simultaneously recalls other constructed landscapes such as Piper's mound at Drottningholm and the burial mounds of Gamla Uppsala, in addition to natural places with the same qualities. Unlike the older precedents, however, there is no specific memorial for one person. So, in this respect, visitors are free to assign their own meanings.

One of these could relate to the human body. As already mentioned, all of the slopes around the perimeter of the mound are variable. In particular, the slope that traces the diagonal from Monument Hall to the Meditation Grove is irregular, with more pronounced bumps, as one might see in a breast or knee. The staircase and gravel path that ascend the knoll, while having a more regular gradient, are recessed into the earth, like a cleft in a body (Figure 5.15). Though Lewerentz is credited with proposing the knoll and Meditation Grove, there is a far more extensive record in Asplund's work of forms that evoke parts of the body. The balusters at the Lister Courthouse, the fireplace at Stennäs, and the light fixtures at the Monument Hall are among the more obvious examples. Though it is possible to attribute these references to an abiding interest in Vitalism on Asplund's part, he never acknowledged it in any writing. Vitalism, as previously mentioned, was a widespread movement in both the sciences and arts in the late nineteenth and early twentieth centuries that stemmed in large part from the influence of Nietzsche's *The Birth of Tragedy*. It was intended to reorient the creative arts towards instinct and the body and away from purely cerebral pursuits. As is the case with the *Angel of Death*, the nature of Vitalism allowed Asplund to easily align it with pre-Christian beliefs, leading to ambiguous identities that are simultaneously modern and archaic.

Wrede has suggested an even earlier source for Vitalism in the works of Northern Romantic painters of the early nineteenth century, Caspar David Friedrich in particular.[4] It was these painters who originally portrayed a new Christian intensity in the landscape, inspiring a later generation, including Munch, Nolde, and Van Gogh. From this perspective, Vitalism can be seen as a more modern incarnation of an already existing tendency in the arts of northern countries. The emphasis, Rosenblum observes, is different in the later generation where natural powers "often become eroticized, so that the malevolent destinies of Romantic avalanches and storms or the exhilarating terror of isolation in a boundless landscape could be translated into an awareness of some overwhelming sexual force, emanating from nature, which dominated human behavior and reduced man to helplessness" (Rosenblum 1975, 110).

Beyond its different interpretations, it is worth considering how the Meditation Grove might be used. For most of those coming and going to a memorial service, it is obviously a striking presence seen from the Way of the Cross and the Memorial Hall. In addition to the ambiguities associated with its form and histories, most would see it as a place to go alone. The reality is that the majority of those attending services do not actually visit there.[5] This could be called an imagined use, where bereaved visitors would place themselves in the Meditation Grove without actually going there. In this way it serves as reminder that, despite the catharsis of the memorial service, mourning must be faced alone. As an imagined place, seen from a distance, it also functions as an invitation to return to the cemetery later to remember the service and the deceased.

FIGURE 5.14 View from Meditation Grove, Woodland Cemetery, Lewerentz, 1924–40

Source: Author photo

FIGURE 5.15 View of staircase to Meditation Grove looking north, Woodland Cemetery, Lewerentz, 1924–40

Source: Author photo

Despite its limited use by those attending services, there is no doubt that Asplund wished to put it in relationship with the Monument Hall. Though it is difficult to assign exact responsibility between Asplund and Lewerentz, the grade was reformed at the southeast of the Meditation Grove to emphasize a diagonal axis towards the ceremonial plaza or "Hill of Repose" and the Monument Hall (see Figure 5.10). Development drawings show how Asplund struggled for a number of years over the best relationship between these elements. There is a critical undated drawing that shows the final version, a diagonal alignment, drawn over a rectilinear one (Figure 5.16). This is when he inserted a lily pond and the Hill of Repose in one axis as seen from Monument Hall. Though this move is understated, it shows a reuse of the diagonal view as a primary perspective that occurs at the Stadsbibliotek and the Stockholm Exhibition.

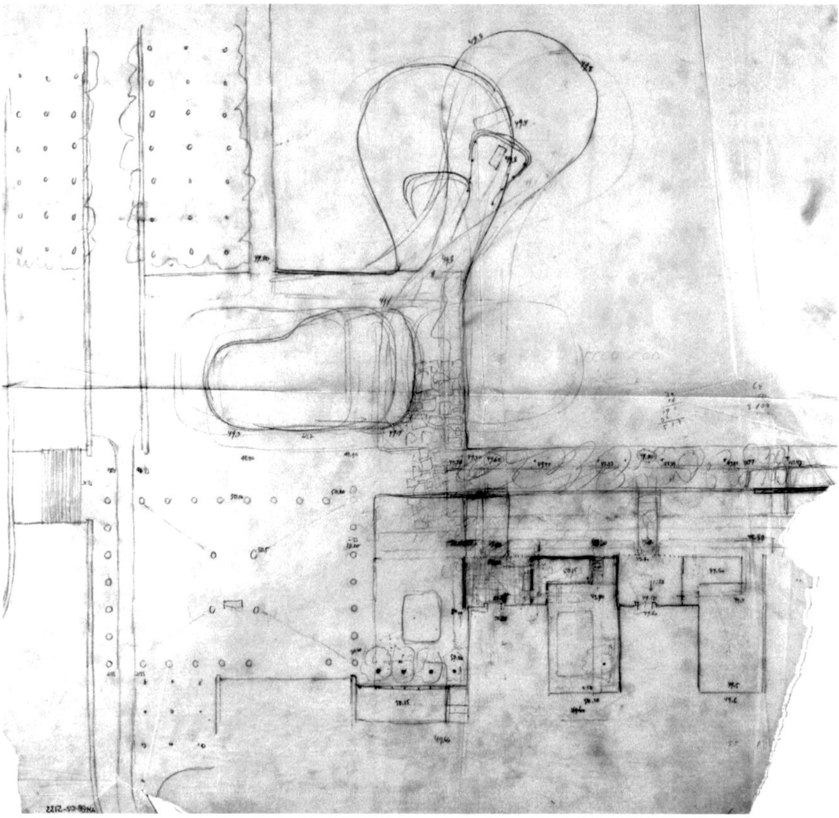

FIGURE 5.16 Sketch of Woodland Crematorium showing Hill of Repose, Woodland Cemetery, Asplund, circa 1935

Source: The Swedish Center for Architecture and Design, ARKM.1988-02-5133

In both of these cases the reflecting pool was an important part of the view. At Observatorielunden it serves as a focal point for the park; it both appeals to a tendency to stare at the changing qualities of water and the impulse of small children and dogs to play in it. In addition, the library, seen from the south entry to the park, is beautifully presented as a reflection in the pool. He appears to have had a similar motive at the Stockholm Exhibition, where a small pond was made along the Corso, so the Paradise Restaurant and exhibition pavilions could be seen in the same way.

While it has some qualities in common with these precedents, his agenda for this reflecting pool at the Woodland Cemetery is somewhat different. It is located between the small outdoor ceremonial plaza with torches called the Hill of Repose and the Monument Hall at the crest of the hill (see Figure 5.4). By acting as an obstacle, it serves to make a meaningful journey for the path that bends around the pond to the ceremonial plaza. This diagonal relationship between pond, plaza, and hall also includes the Mediation Grove, which lies on the same axis. As a result, the Monument Hall is beautifully reflected, or seems to float, when looking from the plaza or Meditation Grove and vice versa (see Figure 5.10). A floating impression is enhanced by islands of lily pads. In this way, by simply acting as a mirror to the sky, the pond becomes a tableau for all kinds of impressions, phenomena, and interpretations.

This axis is important because the Meditation Grove and the Monument Hall (and chapels) speak about two kinds of origins and two kinds of mourning. The Meditation Grove isolates the individual and provides the solace of the distant view and the open sky. The crematorium, meanwhile, presents itself as a fragment of urbanism and speaks of the strength of community when facing bereavement. At either end of the axis, Asplund wants the other to be within view or evoked. This is roughly analogous to the experience at the top of Observatoriekullen, where Asplund was careful to carve out a visual corridor to make an individual aware of the lively community life below. On the one hand, this visual access gives an imaginative release to another place or state of mind, suggesting that the architect thought that both community and individual reflection should be part of mourning. On the other, the presence of one place serves to concretely define the other.

Whether mourning alone or with others, the architect clearly also wished to encourage speculation about the importance of origins. Perhaps the most obvious reason is that a consciousness of origins is an escape from Christian orthodoxy, and, in this respect, it is ironically modern.[6] While this modernity reflects the rapid decline of Christianity in Sweden in the early twentieth century, it also serves to reconnect the bereaved, however superficially, with spiritual traditions that derive directly from worship of the natural world. In the sweeping landscape of the North Entry, this effort can be seen as a form of nationalism, as it reintroduces spiritual beliefs from pre-Christian Sweden.

Another attempt to introduce origins, both nationalist and religious, can be seen in the planting very close to the axis of Monument Hall and the Meditation Grove. At some point soon after 1932, Asplund began to develop an idea for a forest of birch trees (*Betula pendula*) planted in a grid at the top of the hill just beyond the crematorium and before the pine forest (see Figure 5.1).[7] This was primarily intended to receive a looping road, coming from behind the crematorium, which crosses under the compluvium for dropping off those attending services. Clearly, this was designed to offer some experience of landscape for those who do not walk up the Way of the Cross. On one level, there is a latent nationalism because it is a characteristic tree in the Swedish countryside. On another, as a tenacious pioneer species, it is the first tree to grow after devastation, so it is known as the tree of new beginnings. In addition, birch twigs are used in Swedish homes at Easter time as a symbol of resurrection or penance. Finally, it is a distinctly modern idea to design a landscape for the speed and perspective of an occupant of a car. Just as those who approach the Hill of Repose must go around a pond, a car has a forest as a transition.

The birch forest planted in a grid had a relationship to early versions of the crematorium that featured a forest of columns as a portico. There were also versions with discrete porticos for each chapel. Asplund experimented with several versions of this scheme that stretched the portico the full width of the crematorium and several bays deep.[8] One of these schemes even featured trees planted on an offset grid within the columns, suggesting a roof that would filter light. This was perhaps a too literal translation of the tree-to-column relationship present at the Woodland Chapel and Liselund, but it does reveal an intention. Another version of this thinking proposed a forest of columns in front of three chapels designed with curving walls facing west; entry to the chapels in this context would take place between them (Figure 5.17).

Besides the birch forest, the other landscape relationship that preoccupied Asplund was that of the columbaria immediately north along the Way of the Cross. The columbaria were planned to alternate between denser groups of parallel walls and open courts. He worked through one version where east-to-west walls that derive from the columbaria also form chapels and courts for the crematorium (Figure 5.18). Effectively, the architecture was to arise from the order of a garden. Another related version shows the columbaria formed by an architectural order where they are configured as landscaped rooms, suggesting ruins (Figure 5.19).

In most of these cases, there are layered purposes where functional needs and the desire to relate to or reference landscape become part of the same agenda. For example, a primary consideration was the need for waiting areas. Asplund calculated that all those attending services would be spending time to gather or wait quietly both before and after the service. Judging by the attention he gives to this problem, he must have felt that this time was just as important as the service itself. The portico, for example, allows generous space to gather and a position to view the sweeping landscape. It also permitted a visual relationship to the grid of birch trees to the southwest of the crematorium. Of course, those waiting in cars to drop off the bereaved would also pass through the birch forest before arriving at the portico. Finally, the idea of an interior courtyard both allowed a relationship to the columbaria and offered a more private place to wait.

In the final scheme, Asplund is able to respect both the birch forest and the columbaria in equal measure, wedding landscape and function. The form of each chapel is articulated from the Way of the Cross, with small forecourts serving the purpose of the formerly continuous portico (Figure 5.20). The smaller ones are named the Chapel of Faith and the Chapel of Hope, while the larger one is called the Chapel of the Holy Cross. It lies at the top of the hill, using the Monument Hall as its forecourt. Once more Asplund allows different choices for the problem of waiting. There are small canopies on either side of the forecourts that allow some shelter for those committed to waiting outside the door of the chapel (see Figure 5.8). There are also the private courts with small loggias that connect directly to them, as well as interior waiting rooms for those who prefer them (Figure 5.21). In the rear there is a simple bar building in the Functionalist style where coffins are delivered to the different chapels on lifts (Figure 5.22). After a

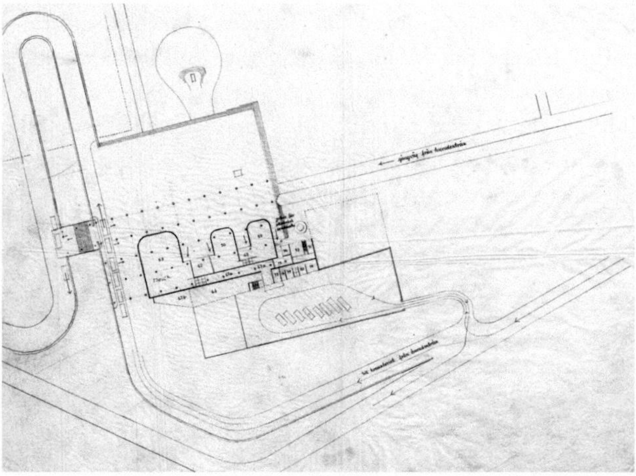

FIGURE 5.17 Schematic design with forest of columns, Woodland Crematorium, Asplund, early thirties

Source: The Swedish Center for Architecture and Design, ARKM. 1988-02-5652HE

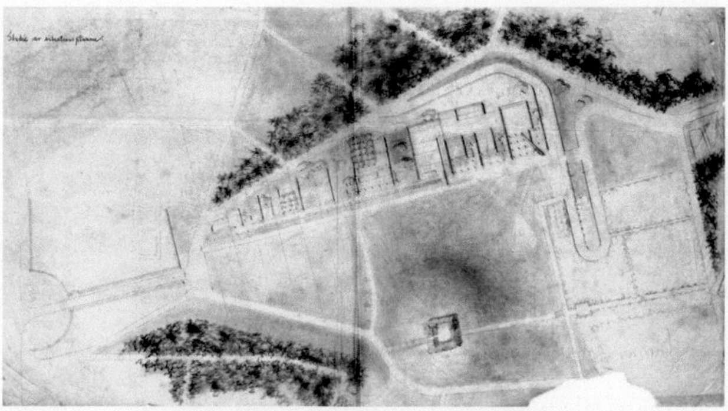

FIGURE 5.18 Columbaria walls scheme, Woodland Crematorium, Asplund, early thirties

Source: The Swedish Center for Architecture and Design, ARKM. 1988-02-5118

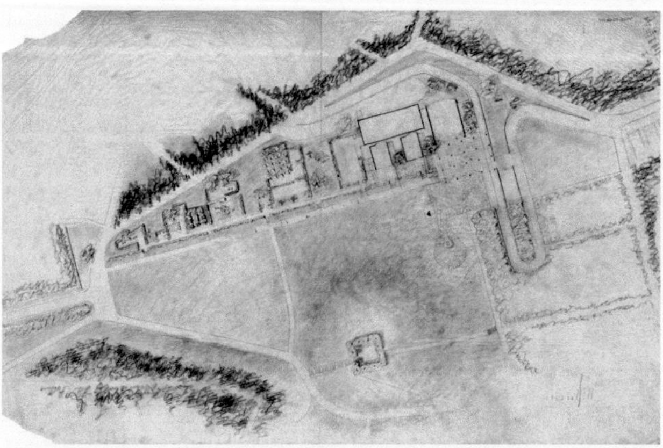

FIGURE 5.19 Garden room scheme, Woodland Crematorium, Asplund, early thirties

Source: The Swedish Center for Architecture and Design, ARKM. 1988-02-5232

service, the coffin descends to the crematorium level. There was concern expressed about the symbolism of this descent, but Asplund insisted that if all those attending had left, there would be no cause for concern (Constant 1994, 93).

The Chapel of the Holy Cross is symmetrical, with a three-sided peristyle with architrave and stone columns (Figure 5.23). The floor is made of a radiating stone pattern that extends out into the floor of the Monument Hall, blurring the line between inside and outside. This was accomplished even more forcefully by a curtain wall facade, facing the Monument Hall, that was to retract into the floor.[9] The ceiling is high, with clerestory windows on the south side. The walls and ceiling are gently curved. This panoramic quality accommodates the mural and, as Elias Cornell comments, is one of many examples of an evocation of the sky by Asplund (1986, 22–33). The floor, flush with the outdoors, slopes gently down towards the catafalque and lift where the coffin is positioned. Meanwhile, there is a stone wainscot that marks a grade line within the chapel. This is not to be confused with the horizon line in the mural by Sven Erixson, which is considerably higher. One interpretation is that one has already entered an excavation; on one hand, this could be related to interment, while on the other, it could be archeological. In other words, the descent to another stratum in the ground is also a passage in time to a level where a temple or peristyle has a footing. Yet another interpretation relates to the Hill of Repose and the ceremonial plaza outdoors. Here the slope of the ground is a close match to that which exists in the Chapel of the Holy Cross. In addition, this reading is reinforced by the close similarity in shape and scale of the footprint of the plaza to that of the chapel. While all readings are equally valid, it is even more important to point out that the outdoor and indoor places provide a cross reference; one is free to bring an impression of the outside to the inside and vice versa.

The smaller chapels, named "Hope" and "Faith," are more intimate and rectangular. Each is asymmetrical, with a partial peristyle on one side. Lighting comes from clerestory windows that face south. The floors have muted patterns and gently slope towards the altar and catafalque (Figure 5.24). The small courtyards, meanwhile, have an understated residential quality, with stone paths and shrubs on the perimeter (see Figure 5.21). The loggias at one end represent a partial peristyle, a fragment of the original model.

The chapels are all designed to present large-scale works of art, including bas-relief, fresco, and mosaic. Although they differ in quality, there is an underlying intention to associate contemporary people with landscapes and supernatural beings, including angels and biblical figures. The Chapel of the Holy Cross has a large fresco by Sven Erixson that portrays a ship sailing for the horizon while groups of figures, standing on small hills, watch it from the coast (see Figure 5.23). A less demonstrative approach is used in the Chapel of Faith, where there are bas-relief figures by Ivar Johnsson of field workers reaping wheat and an angel receiving a departed soul in the light of the clerestory. From an artistic and political point of view, the most revealing is the mosaic in the Chapel of Hope by Otto Sköld (see Figure 5.24). It shows modern urban people and farmers under a large tree.

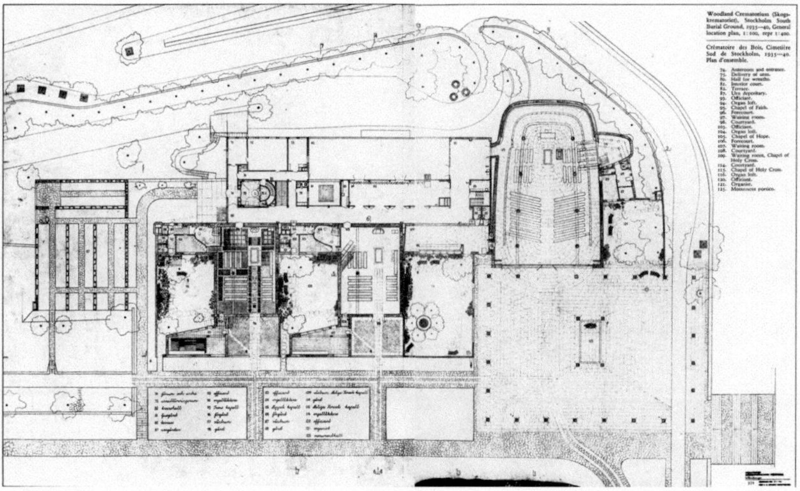

FIGURE 5.20 Final plan for Woodland Crematorium, Asplund, circa 1935

Source: G. Holmdahl, S. Lind., K. Ödeen (eds), *Gunnar Asplund Architect*, Stockholm, Sweden: A B Tibskriften Byggmästaren, 1950

FIGURE 5.21 View of courtyard and Chapel of Faith, Asplund, Woodland Crematorium, 1933–40

Source: C. G. Rosenberg photo, The Swedish Center for Architecture and Design, ARKM.1988-104-0671

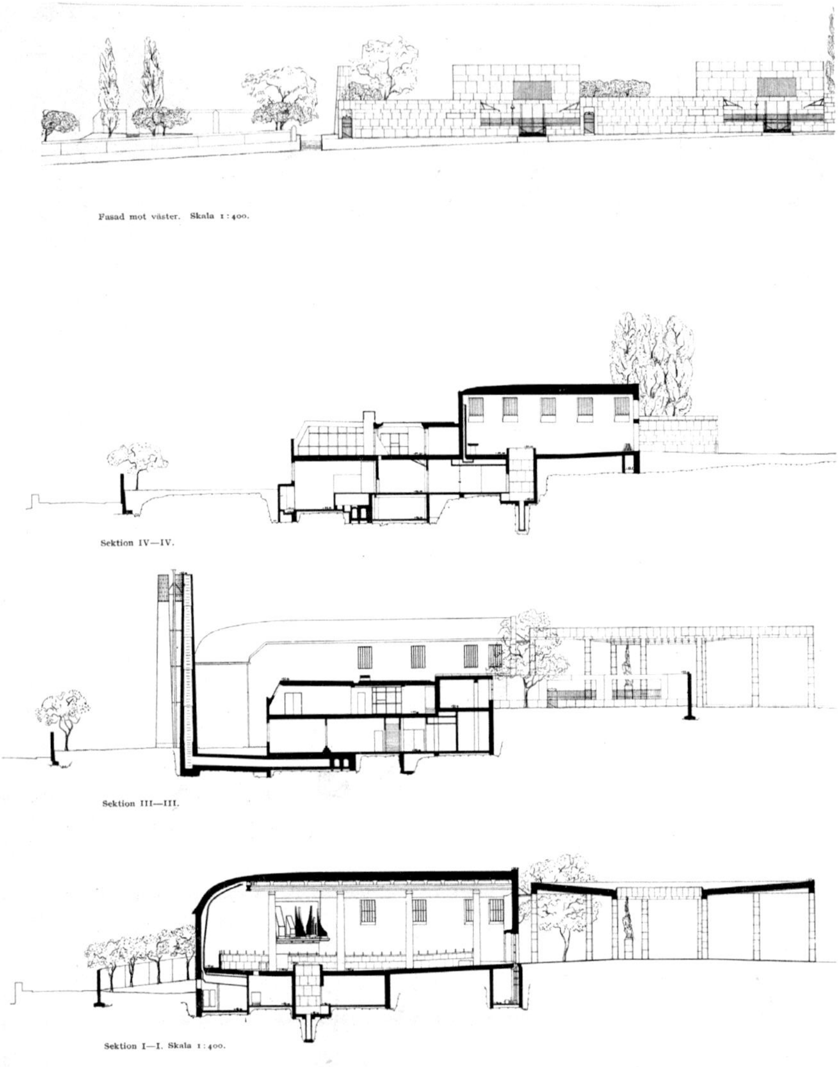

FIGURE 5.22 Sections and elevation of Woodland Crematorium, Asplund, circa 1935

Source: The Swedish Center for Architecture and Design, ARKM.1962-101-1163

FIGURE 5.23 Chapel of the Holy Cross Interior, Asplund, Woodland Crematorium, 1933–40

Source: C. G. Rosenberg photo, The Swedish Center for Architecture and Design, ARKM. 1988-104-0677

FIGURE 5.24 Interior of Chapel of Hope, Woodland Crematorium, Asplund, 1935–40

Source: C. G. Rosenberg photo, The Swedish Center for Architecture and Design, ARKM. 1994-112-5122

They share the company of a figure in ancient attire, and all are gazing towards an unknown horizon. It can read as a portrait of the alliance between working people and farmers, the backbone of the Social Democrats' coalition. A more significant interpretation would relate to Asplund's intention to connect the bereaved with ancient forms of spirituality and the natural world.

This intention is even more evident in Asplund's borrowings from Roman domestic architecture. The Roman house represents a composite of landscape and dwelling, integrating a garden in the house. In his journals from his visit to Pompeii as a young man, Asplund expressed delight with the scale and sequence of a courtyard, an impluvium, and a peristyle in a Roman house. He mentions that the qualities are "comfortable middle class" in comparison with antique monumental buildings and Renaissance palaces (Ahlberg 1950, 26). The House of the Faun in Pompeii, for example, has peristyles and atria of all sizes, where some are related to public functions while others are dedicated to family life (Figure 5.25). Eccentric axes and cross axes unified indoors and outdoors spaces together, offering prospects from living spaces to a sunlight and planting. Though urban, often with shops next to the front door, it is also served as a virtual temple to gods of landscape and to ancestors (the *lares*). Life masks of ancestors were displayed in shrines, and frescos of gardens typically decorated the walls. This was also the scene of funeral rites, where a body was laid on the ground and anointed. The funeral procession would depart from the home to a cemetery on the edge of town where cremation would take place (Clarke 1991, 2–19).

There is no sense of a literal transcription of a Roman house at the crematorium. Instead, Asplund engages in a process of transformation of familiar elements. Monument Hall is a peristyle turned into a compluvium. Instead of an inward-looking space, it becomes a place of reception that frames the landscape around it. In particular, it serves as an architectural counterpoint to the Meditation Grove beyond. Another form of peristyle, the columns and architrave in the Chapel of the Holy Cross, is meanwhile condensed to evoke the outdoors. Curiously, unlike the Roman house, where public rooms enjoyed visual access to gardens and atria, the chapels at the crematorium do not allow any view to the neighboring courts. One can speculate that this was done to segregate the funeral service from a place of waiting or contemplation. In addition, a view of a court would distract from the evocation of the outside in the large artworks.

References to antiquity, however, do more than offer an escape from Christian orthodoxy. They also allow an unusual view of space and time. Because the Stockholm Exhibition and the Woodland Cemetery are both enhanced and

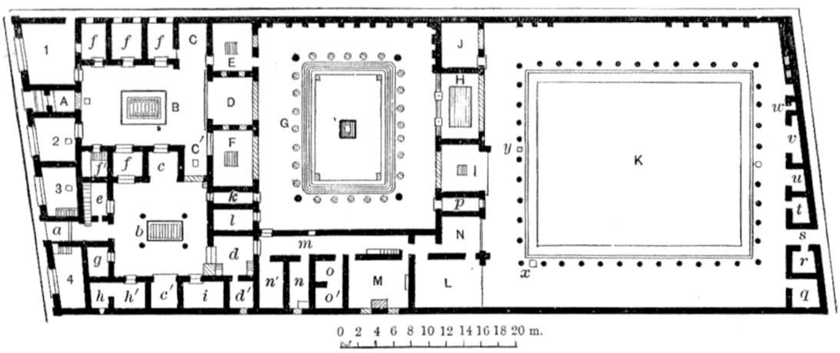

Fig. 137.—Plan of the house of the Faun.

A. Fauces of Tuscan atrium.
B. Tuscan atrium.
C, C'. Alae.
D. Tablinum.
E, F. Dining rooms.
G. First peristyle.
H. Exedra with mosaic of the battle of Alexander.
I, J. Dining rooms.
K. Second peristyle.
L. Large room used as wine-cellar.
M. Kitchen.
N. Bedroom.
a. Vestibule.
b. Tetrastyle atrium.
c, *c'*. Alae of tetrastyle atrium.
e. Storeroom.
f, *f'*. Sleeping rooms.
o, *o'*. Bath.
q. Gardener's room.
r. Doorkeeper's room.
v. Broad niche for three statues.
1–4. Shops.

FIGURE 5.25 Plan of the House of the Faun, Pompeii, second century BC

Source: August Mau, *Pompeii: Its Life and Art*, London: Macmillan, 1907

segregated versions of the everyday world with special purposes, they too can be considered variations of Foucault's understanding of the heterotopia already mentioned (Foucault 2001). Both can also be classified as heterotopias of time, where the Stockholm Exhibition embraces an ephemeral vision of the future, while the Woodland Cemetery serves as a gateway to eternity. In the latter case, with its layered references to different eras and simulated artifacts, it also has much in common with the library or museum, other heterotopias of time. Because of this encyclopedic quality, the experience of the bereaved can be a distinctive understanding of time and space. They have the chance of assuming the perspective that Freud discusses in *Civilization and Its Discontents*, where he attempts to explain the simultaneous existence of older and newer parts of human consciousness. Here, he portrays this coexistence as a vision of ancient Rome where all buildings are intact but overlapping. "Now let us, by flight of imagination, suppose that Rome is not a human habitation but a psychical entity with a similarly long and copious past—an entity, that is to say, in which nothing that has once come into existence will have passed away and all the earlier phases of development continue to exist alongside the latest one" (1961, 17).

Asplund and Lewerentz perform this feat of simultaneity through facsimiles of ancient buildings within modern ones while also creating the illusion of infinite space. For example, the Roman peristyle lies embedded in the Chapel of the Holy Cross, and the Pantheon lies within the diminutive Woodland Chapel. They also accomplish this through overlapping references. The Iron Age burial mound, for example, lies within the swelling breast shape of the Meditation Grove, and the earth goddess lies within the *Angel of Death*. Some might see this as an analogy with our own psyche; following Freud's theory of the coexistence of early and modern parts of our consciousness, just as the temple survives within the modern chapel, pantheistic religion survives within all of us. One implication is that all the bereaved are brought together by this persistence of human memory (Cornell 1986, 33).

This particular insight may not strike everyone at once. Instead, the visit at the North Entry should be seen as an unfolding process. For those coming to the Woodland Cemetery for the first time to attend a service, the initial experience of the open landscape is a preliminary introduction. One might expect that three messages might be imparted. The stone path suggests that "others have walked this path before." The Meditation Grove announces that "this is an excellent place to be alone when the time comes." Finally, the clock says that "your time here is short as well." The architecture of the chapels, particularly the Chapel of the Holy Cross, continues to deliver messages, but in a different way. It functions as a theatre of imagination; through speeches, art, and architecture the bereaved are quietly instructed about forming a story about the loss of the loved one. The mural in the Chapel of the Holy Cross, for example, asks you to imagine death as a departure on the sea to an unknown place, while the architecture speaks about the open sky and the presence of ancient rituals. When the service is over, the landscape presents itself as a refuge for the individual where a story about loss and present life can continue to form and the same themes about landscape and its cultural presence can be revisited. In this way, the North Entry treats mourning as a theatrical event that introduces the bereaved to the long process that it will become. Here, landscape serves as a prelude, then a leitmotif, and finally a long-term presence.

This solace of landscape could have been some consolation for Swedes whose lives were very different from those of their parents and grandparents. In the first four decades of the twentieth century, Sweden underwent astonishing change. In 1900, it was a backwater with a constitutional monarchy and limited franchise. By 1940, when the Woodland crematorium was finished, it was a prosperous, industrialized state with a popular socialist government. Because of this significant change in less than one generation, the majority of Swedes, formerly with strong rural roots, were adjusting to urban existence. The doctrine of the Stockholm School of landscape design, mentioned in the introduction, brought together modern housing blocks and new parks in the forties and addressed this native discomfort with urban existence.[10] The final phase of the Woodland Cemetery, with the Stockholm Exhibition as a prelude, attempted to embody this new urban ideal as a series of courtyards, on the edge of a surreal version of an English common. In this respect, the sweeping open space at the Woodland Cemetery draws on the memory of Drottningholm, Haga, and the Stockholm park. The equilibrium in the everyday between memory and modernism was translated to a place of death.

This translation was largely accomplished through the use of modern design. It allowed Asplund and Lewerentz to reframe ancient concepts of body, landscape, and the Cosmos in modern terms. In the process, they left open a range of interpretation, thereby welcoming Swedes of different beliefs. It also made an appropriate setting for cremation, a method that could be efficient, hygienic, and culturally meaningful. Finally, it permitted a design that emphasizes landscape more than architecture. The versatility of this expression signified that modernism was not a fashion of the moment in Sweden. Instead, as a polemic, the last phase of the Woodland Cemetery is a built epilogue to the *acceptera* manifesto and the Stockholm Exhibition.

This was a different form of modernism, however, than that imagined by Functionalist ideologues. It proved that it could offer durable solutions to real problems, both cultural and technical, and speak of the present *and* the past. According to this approach, present and future are found not through ruthless efficiency, but through a broader view of function that can include choices and calculated ambiguity. The past, meanwhile, is used analytically to serve modern beliefs and agendas. Landscape was the agent behind this approach. It offered the underlying nationalist consensus as well as the necessary nuances to please all parties. It also provided the required monumentality that realized the promise of the Tallum scheme and enshrined the centrality of the individual's grief.

Notes

1 Adam von Bremen was a Franconian and the first historian to document the activity of the archbishops of Hamburg-Bremen and the geography of Northern Europe in the second part of the eleventh century.
2 The other large project by Piper, previously mentioned, is Haga Park, near Solna. Like Drottningholm Park, it also has a network of pavilions, linked by diagonal site lines. The primary place, the Great Pelouse, is an enormous bowl-like space that descends to the Brunnsviken. Though three buildings, including the Copper Tents by Desprez, were built on the perimeter, the Great Pelouse exists autonomously.
3 This information was provided by Niklas Edell, landscape architect of the Woodland Cemetery.
4 This opinion was expressed in correspondence with the author. Wrede suggests the possible influence of Friedrich on Asplund in "Landscape and Architecture: Classical and Vernacular by Asplund," in *Asplund*, eds Claes Caldenby and Oluf Hultin (New York: Rizzoli, 1986) 43. He also stresses the importance of the Northern Romantic painters in "The Garden in the Anthropocene Era," in *The Garden of Life*, ed. Karin Sidén (Stockholm, Sweden: Prins Eugens Waldemarsudde, 2014).
5 This is confirmed by correspondence with Niklas Edell.
6 This is analogous to Strindberg's hero in *By the Open Sea* who contemplates the stars at Christmastime at the end of the novel. He reflects on all cultural meanings, including Christian ones and ancient ones. He arrives at the end at the idea of "a new Christmas star" which he associates with the sea, "the All-mother, in whose lap was kindled the first spark of life" (Strindberg 1913, 324).
7 Edell relates that the original birch forest has been replanted in three stages. The last stage, the outermost layer, is replanted with *Betula pendula* "Youngii".
8 Of the Asplund projects covered here, the Woodland crematorium required the greatest number of variations before it assumed its final form. In this study, I can only draw attention to the most representative versions. Asplund laboriously explored each one using plans, sections, details, and perspectives. These are well documented at ArkDes (The Swedish Center for Architecture and Design) and deserve a dedicated study.
9 Because of an unreliable mechanism, this wall has only been retracted once in 1940, at Asplund's funeral, soon after the opening of the crematorium. See Constant 1994, 193n26.
10 Erik Bülow Hübe also carried out this agenda in multiple projects in Malmö. See Arne Wittstrand, *Stadens Landskap: Erik Bülow Hübe och Malmö* (Stockholm, Sweden: Carlssons, 2007).

References

Ahlberg, Hakon. 1950. "Gunnar Asplund Architect." In *Gunnar Asplund Architect, 1885–1940*, edited by Gustav Holmdahl, Sven Ivar Lind, and Kjell Ödeen, 9–81. Stockholm, Sweden: A. B. Tidskriften Byggmästaren.

Bauer, Walter. 1981. "F. M. Piper at Drottningholm." In *Fredrik Magnus Piper och den Romantiska Parken*, edited by Karin Lindegren, 39–53. Stockholm, Sweden: Royal Academy of Fine Arts.

Bremen, Adam von. 1959. *History of the Archbishops of Hamburg-Bremen*. New York: Columbia University Press.

Childs, Marquis. 1947. *Sweden: The Middle Way*. New Haven, CT: Yale University Press.

Clarke, John. 1991. *The Houses of Roman Italy, 100 BC–AD 250: Ritual, Space, and Decoration*. Berkeley, CA: University of California Press.

Constant, Caroline. 1994. *The Woodland Cemetery: Toward a Spiritual Landscape*. Stockholm, Sweden: Byggförlaget.

Cornell, Elias. 1986. "The Sky as a Vault." In *Asplund*, edited by Claes Caldenby and Oluf Hultin, 22–33. New York: Rizzoli.

Foucault, Michel. 2001. "Des Espaces autres." In *Dits et écrits*, edited by Daniel Defert and François Ewald, 1571–81. Paris, France: Gallimard.

Freud, Sigmund. 1961. *Civilization and Its Discontents*. New York: W. W. Norton.

Rosenblum, Robert. 1975. *Modern Painting and the Northern Romantic Tradition*. New York: Harper and Row.

Sporrong, Ulf. 2008. "The Regional Identity of Historical Sweden." In *Nordic Landscapes: Region and Belonging on the Northern Edge of Europe*, edited by Michael Jones and Kenneth Olwig, 141–56. Minneapolis, MN: University of Minnesota Press.

Strindberg, August. 1913. *By the Open Sea*. Translated by Ellie Schleussner. New York: B. W. Huebsch.

Tilton, Tim. 1990. *The Political Theory of Swedish Social Democracy*. Oxford: Oxford University Press.

Wickman, Kerstin. 1998. "Homes." In *Sweden: Twentieth Century Architecture*, edited by Claes Caldenby, Jöran Lindvall, and Wilfried Wang, 198–225. Munich, Germany: Prestel.

6

LANDSCAPE AND SUMMERHOUSE AT STENNÄS

A Vitalist poem

A visitor to the Stockholm Exhibition in 1930 might have come away with the impression that a Functionalist summerhouse should be efficient and white, with plenty of south-facing windows. The same visitor might be surprised that Asplund defied this formula when he built his own summerhouse on an inlet south of Stockholm at Stennäs in 1938. Though white, his house has no ribbon windows or flat roofs. It does not loudly proclaim the advent of a new age like the model homes at the exhibition. Instead, it presents a mix of intentions; it is simultaneously vernacular, modern, and idiosyncratic. Pure Functionalism has been eschewed in favor of a heterogeneous approach where both landscape design and architecture declare mixed origins and where the highest priority is placed on the continuity of landscape and culture. Here, the design is also animated by a Vitalist agenda that attempts to associate body, architecture, and landscape. This can be understood as a different form of humanism, where insight appears to derive from a poetic view of the natural world and Swedish culture rather than mastery of the classical arts or complete acceptance of machine production.

Fortunately, the site has the necessary qualities to be worthy of this agenda. It is decidedly rural in a region at the far southern edge of the geography of the Stockholm archipelago or Skärgård (Figure 6.1), a relatively unusual coastal landscape formed by a complex network of fault lines. Glaciers exploited weak spots in the gneiss, granite, leptite, and limestone geology to hollow out multiple small valleys, most of which have since filled with organic material and vegetation. The landform is thus a mirror image of the dense network of small coastal islands or skerries, where the valleys are filled with water (Hedenstierna 1960, 4–7). In other words, the multiple outcrops that exist on the site immediately to the north are dry-land counterparts to the skerries off the coast, a remarkably dense network of small and large islands.

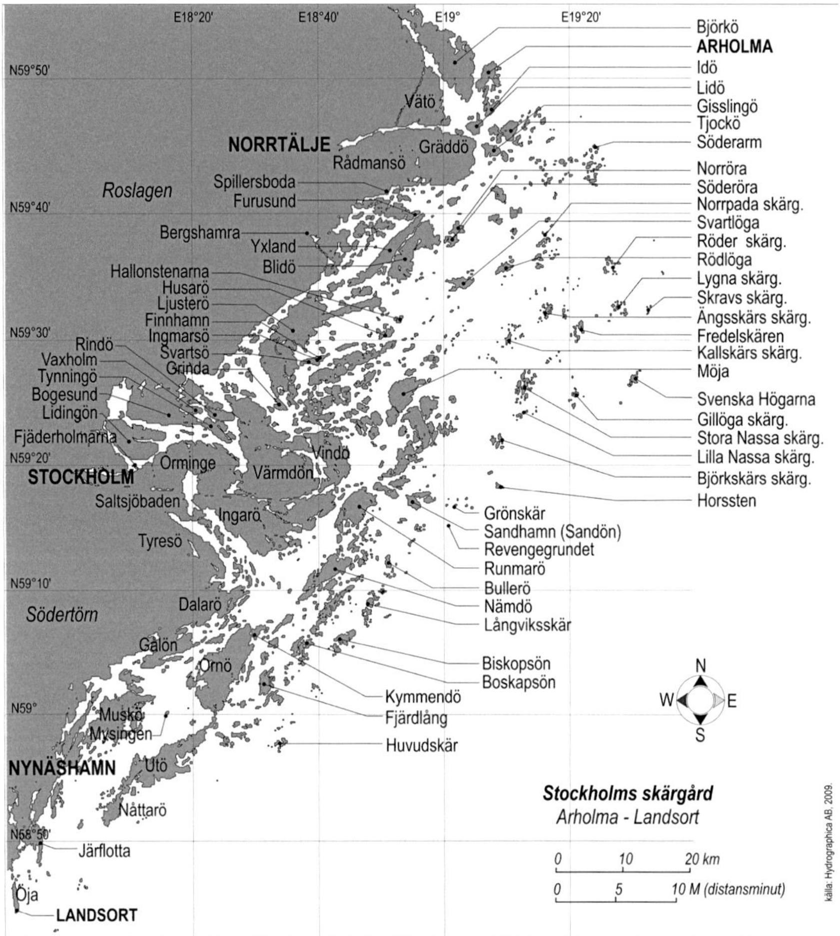

FIGURE 6.1 Map of Stockholm archipelago

Source: Hydrographica AB, 2009

This region has been occupied for centuries by fisherman and farmers eking out a difficult living. In the last century, the native population declined as opportunities in the nearby metropolis increased. Meanwhile, this idyllic landscape of equal parts sea and land has become the most convenient leisure destination for Stockholm residents. In the early twentieth century, those seeking a respite would rent a house from a farmer or fishermen. Later, it became more usual for these people to own their own second homes (Hedenstierna 1960, 16–24).

As a result of this new trend, there was much interest in the *sportstuga*, or small country house, in the early thirties (Jones 2006, 192). Asplund, in fact, was a juror for a competition for one in 1933. Soon after, he attempted to design one himself. It was very simple, with a strong Functionalist imprint, but the furniture is lovingly detailed and there is the latent presence of the old farmhouse in the corner fireplace and the built-in box beds. At about the same time, he received a commission to design a small weekend house for the southeast coast of Sweden for a client named Bäckström. It features two simple forms, one flat-roofed with servant spaces and the other with a pitched roof that houses a living room. As Jones observes, the critical part is a skewed fireplace that links the two parts (193). Though the house lacked a strong response to the landscape, in the late thirties, when Asplund began to take an interest in building a summerhouse for himself, this idea would reemerge.

His family had become familiar with a peninsula near Sorunda, forty miles south of Stockholm. Here, Asplund purchased a large coastal parcel at the head of an inlet that included rocky outcrops, a narrow swath of gently sloping ground, as well as a broad salt marsh. What made this opportunity particularly extraordinary was Asplund's ability to select his own site and make decisions without having to cater to the needs and tastes of a client. A Functionalist approach to this design would have dictated a long east/west axis where all rooms would enjoy sunlight and view. Following this strategy, the site would have been divided into front and back. Instead, Asplund preferred to preserve the continuity of the landscape from hilltop to the water by deciding to orient the house on a north/south axis. He did this, however, in an unusual way. First, his primary decision was to place the rear corner of the house in relation to the corner of an outcrop (Figure 6.2). The main axis of the house is then aligned with the eastern edge of the outcrop. Second, a line of trees, walls, and fences peels off from the cliff to define the southern edge and returns on the east side.

The sensitivity of this "necklace" of elements demonstrates how Asplund finds the opportunities within the site so every decision can be linked with an existing condition rather than imposing formal order. In effect, the language of the garden is drawn from the site to the point where there seems to be a seamless or inevitable quality. For example, the dry-laid retaining wall on the south side, made from rounded glacial rocks, is placed in relation to a low wall of glacial rocks. That, in turn, is seen in the context of random glacial boulders in the lawn. Likewise, the schematic site plan indicates that new trees planted by Asplund, fruit-bearing or otherwise, are placed to have a discernible relationship to more mature trees that existed previously. In this way, all interventions are intended to relate to existing qualities of the site.

As a way of discerning a method in Asplund's site planning, it is instructive to refer to an article he wrote for *Arkitektur* in 1916 called "Current Architectural Dangers for Stockholm: Blocks of Flats." Here he expressed a theory of urban contextual design, using an artist's response to a natural scene as a starting point:

> An artist trying to paint a landscape, for example a red cottage on a green field, and who wants to produce an illusory effect, puts a little green from the field into the red colour of the house, and in this way makes the house

FIGURE 6.2 Preliminary Stennäs site plan, Asplund, circa 1936

Source: The Swedish Center Architecture and Design, ARKM.1988-02-10216

> grow softly out of nature. Similarly the architect can make a new building seem to grow naturally out of its environment only by borrowing something from the surrounding buildings—their scale, their materials, their construction or their motifs.
>
> (Jones 2006, 80)

This passage demonstrates how Asplund thought of himself as the creator of illusions. It also suggests how he might think if given an architectural problem where the natural environment becomes the context. In this case, the dialogue then changes to one between architecture and all aspects of the natural environment, including landform, flora, climate, and perhaps time itself.

A previous example of this opportunistic form of site planning can be found in Asplund's Södermalm emergency housing from 1917 (Figure 6.3). This was a very small community of traditionally inspired rowhouses built between two outcrops in a neighborhood of Stockholm. Here, the presence and qualities of the landform are treated for their spatial and sculptural qualities. First, on the north side, the connected houses respond to seemingly random changes in the outcrop and give them spatial meaning. Second, an outcrop is framed by a piazza on the east side in the manner of Sitte, as if it were a church or a civic building. In both cases, landform is given meaning as urban form, or, alternately, urban form is allowed to be read as landform.

This approach might strike many as usual because a garden is the usual intermediary to make a dialogue with a wild landscape possible through contrast and transition. In this typical situation, the domain of the natural world and the limits of the garden are usually quite clear. In the case of Stennäs, however, the garden is found in the way the house collaborates with the outcrop to form a sequence that includes a high point, court, salt marsh, and inlet. Because of this

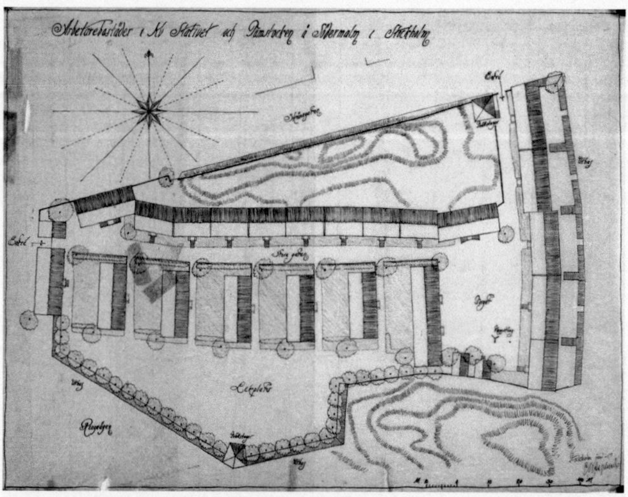

FIGURE 6.3 Södermalm housing site plan, Asplund, 1917

Source: The Center for Swedish Architecture and Design, ARKM. 1988-02-2952-H

mixed origin, it is easy for a reading of the garden spaces to alternate between "untouched meadow" and "courtyard"; like the piazza at Södermalm, these spaces are just as much a base for a compelling outcrop as they are functional areas for the house.

The other aspect of the siting of the house relates to the commanding place where you can see or understand architecture in relation to landscape. At the Woodland Cemetery, you look down from the Meditation Grove to see the chapels and the walk, framed in elms. At the Stadsbibliotek, you look down on the reflecting pool, the rotunda of the library, and the city. In each case, from this place of contemplation, you are able to see an order to the landscape where architecture serves to enhance continuity instead of claiming a role as the center of attention. At Stennäs, likewise, Asplund contrives to site his house to reinforce the sequence of outcrop garden, court, salt marsh, and inlet. He acknowledges that the essential place for viewing is not on a porch or patio or in a living room but on top of the outcrop surveying both what is natural and manmade (Figure 6.4).

The distant view is not the only attraction. After climbing to the top of the outcrop, roughly thirty feet above the lawn, you are greeted with a beautiful rocky landscape where small shrubs and conifers cling to life in pockets of soil between large rocks (Figure 6.5). This is an example of what Thorbjörn Andersson would call a found garden. "To form a garden," he wrote, "has always and with a few exceptions been a question of carefully choosing a place, and rather strengthening and refining its inherent qualities than changing them" (Andersson 1998, 230). This kind of terrain is also characteristic of the landscapes that Rutger Sernander promoted as Swedish archetypes and that Erik Glemme, the city landscape architect, preserved in Stockholm parks.[1]

It is noteworthy that within this conversation of house and outcrop there is no accommodation for the automobile in the site plan near the house. The Transportation Building at the Stockholm Exhibition embraced boats and an airplane in the facade, while trucks and buses were hidden inside. Likewise, a summer place, designed by Erik Friberger for the Leisure Exhibition in Ystad in 1936 (Figure 6.6), raises the living space to an upper story and displays the automobile among columns on the first floor (Rudberg 1998, 99). At Stennäs, however, Asplund had no interest in a prominent display of the automobile. In a preliminary site plan, in fact, the garage is shown at the beginning of a long driveway (see Figure 6.2).

While today it is possible for cars to park somewhat closer than that, it is clear that Asplund wanted the house to be approached on foot along a route where you pass through a small wooded area and then see the side of the house and entrance framed by trees (Figure 6.7). Soon after, the view to the outcrop opens to the left while the view to the salt marsh and the inlet beyond reveals itself to the right. Although this path winds according to the undulation of the landscape, there are several calculated points where there are axial views of the front and rear doors. As you near the house, you pass the end of the aforementioned low stone wall

FIGURE 6.4 View of house and sea from outcrop at Stennäs, Asplund, 1936–38

Source: Author photo

FIGURE 6.5 View of "found garden" at outcrop at Stennäs, Asplund

Source: Author photo

FIGURE 6.6 Summerhouse at Ystad Leisure Exhibition, Erik Friberger, 1936

Source: The Swedish Center of Architecture and Design, ARKM. 1997-110-0602-01

that curves away from the front of the house towards the edge of the outcrop (Figure 6.8). The wall gives the impression of an historic artifact from an earlier occupation. It roughly defines the area where the present owners take their leisure, and, judging from a preliminary site plan (Figure 6.9), this was the intended purpose of this place. Soon after, you pass between the corner of the living room and a large boulder, placed there by Asplund, another threshold in the sequence.

The other outdoor space lies immediately to the left, where there is a wooden door in the meter-wide distance between the corner of the house and the outcrop. This leads to a service area at the rear of the house where the back wall has been recessed to make an open garage for the storage of bicycles and other equipment (Figure 6.10). It also receives a corridor of space along the bottom of the outcrop that ends with a small outbuilding (see Figure 6.2). The underside of the garage roof is painted deep red like the entry porch, the traditional color of Swedish farmhouses. This utilitarian space also serves Asplund's version of the agricultural landscape on the east side of the house, where he grew fruit trees and rows of an unidentified crop (Figure 6.11).

The other secondary outdoor space lies immediately in front of the living room, between the house and the stone wall. This plateau was, no doubt, created by the excavation required for the foundation and footings. A preliminary site plan shows this as the location of a border garden (see Figure 6.9). A detailed plan for such a border garden survives, showing the diversity and color found at the Alnarp garden, but it is not clear that it was ever planted (Figure 6.12). It would have been clearly seen from the living room picture window as a foreground to the boats at the dock and the inlet beyond.

While the site strategy was determined quickly, the design of the house required more time. The record of the development of this house is extremely well documented, thanks to gifts of drawings to the Swedish Museum of Architecture by family members. Many variations exist of the essential concept of the house, and countless versions exist of all details, including fireplace, siding, and structure.

FIGURE 6.7
Distant view of approach at Stennäs, Asplund, 1936–38

Source: Author photo

FIGURE 6.8
View of Approach at Stennäs, Asplund, 1936–38

Source: Author photo

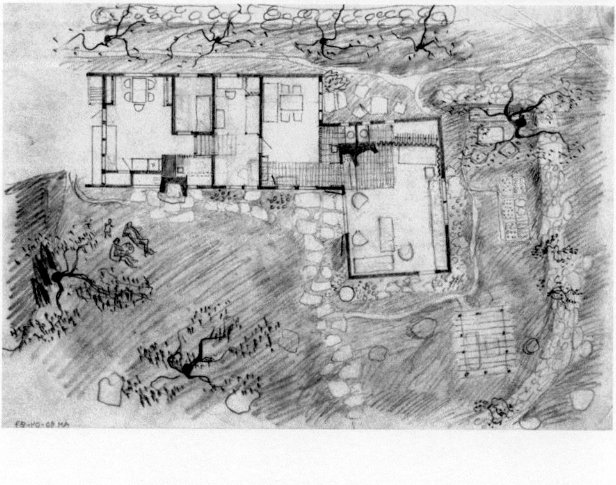

FIGURE 6.9
Floor plan with site plan, Stennäs, Asplund, 1936–38

Source: The Swedish Center for Architecture and Design, ARKM. 1988-04-87

FIGURE 6.10
View of garage looking southwest, Stennäs, Asplund, 1936–38

Source: Author photo

FIGURE 6.11
View of east side looking north, Stennäs, Asplund, 1936–38

Source:
Swedish Center for Architecture and Design, ARKM. 1998-111-00124-A

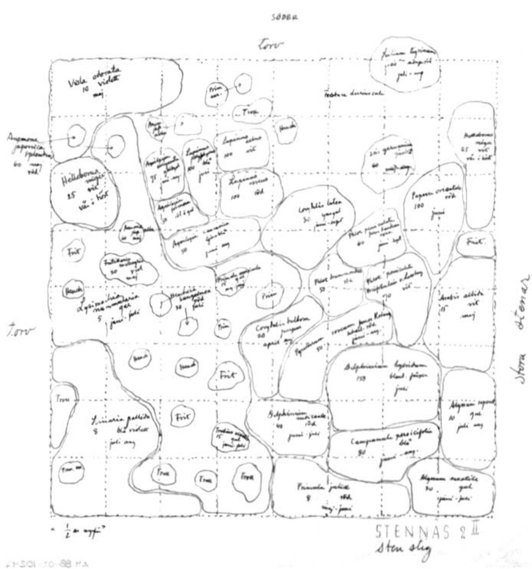

FIGURE 6.12
Planting scheme for border garden, Stennäs, Asplund, 1936–38

Source: The Swedish Center for Architecture and Design, ARKM. 1988-02-10247

Initially, the house was segmented into three parts on different levels with cross-passages (Figure 6.13). This was consistent with an old type of farmhouse, represented by the log structures of the Moragården at Skansen, where smaller stables, barns, and outbuildings surround a courtyard with a dwelling as the main feature (Figure 6.14). Variations exist in Asplund's design development where these three parts are represented with flat roofs with wide siding. Clearly, he wished the house to be very porous, making all parts of the site accessible. At a certain point, he decided in favor of the asymmetrical gabled roof. While increasing the complexity of the plan with four levels, separated by small staircases, he also determined that the mass of the house should be in two parts, a head and a long tail. One can speculate that concerns about thermal comfort and a preference for a stronger axis related to the outcrop prevailed. Effectively, an earlier form of vernacular dwelling lies within the continuous form of a later one, resulting in a simple exterior with a more complicated interior that seamlessly conforms to a sloping landscape (Figure 6.15). This would ensure that the uphill walk from living room to kitchen would be a constant reminder of the slope of the landscape.

The detailing of the exterior of the house is equally nuanced and thoughtful. The wall is made of two-inch planking with siding on the outside and horizontal butted boards on the inside. The horizontal siding is tongue-and-groove and exceptionally narrow at approximately two and one-half inches. From a distance, the joints disappear, and one loses a sense of materiality. At the entrance porch and along the perimeter of the house, this wood siding goes all the way to the ground (Figure 6.16). This runs contrary to good practice in almost any building tradition, Functionalist or vernacular, as a visiting student pointed out (Jones 2006, 199). The only possible conclusion is that Asplund made such a decision for an aesthetic or symbolic purpose.[2] In this case, one can guess that the seamless transition from ground to siding is meant to impart a monolithic quality to the house, suggesting that it sits on the ground like a rock. This theory is more credible in light of the presence of the outcrop and two stones placed in the entry yard. One is a large boulder from nearby that was positioned by Asplund close to the corner of the living room. Another is a broad, flat stone from the Woodland Cemetery that one walks upon when stepping onto the porch (196).

If Asplund wanted a monolithic quality to his house, it is natural to ask why he did not use stone for both foundation and walls. In placing his wood house in relation to a large outcrop and two large stones, he appears to have preferred a poetic exchange of qualities between dissimilar materials rather than literal imitation. It is even more likely that he also intended to create a sense of uncertainty. You are placed in a position to ask what this house is about. Because it is neither completely vernacular nor modern nor natural form, it could be said to be posed between all of these descriptions. Ambiguity in this case does not play a political role; Asplund did not have multiple constituencies to please. Instead, it is a subtle provocation without a fixed interpretation; you are expected to hold them all together—history, body, landscape, and modernism.

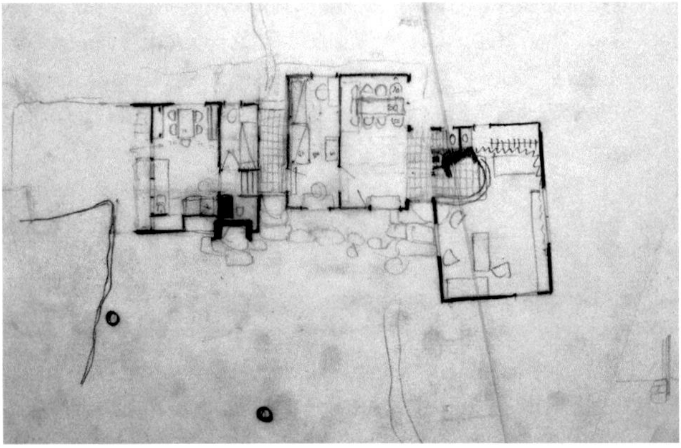

FIGURE 6.13 Three part plan scheme, Stennäs, Asplund, 1936

Source: The Swedish Center for Architecture and Design, ARKM. 1988-02-10128

FIGURE 6.14 Moragården Exterior View, Skansen, Stockholm, buildings date from late seventeenth to late eighteenth centuries, relocated from Mora District in Dalarna

Source: Author photo

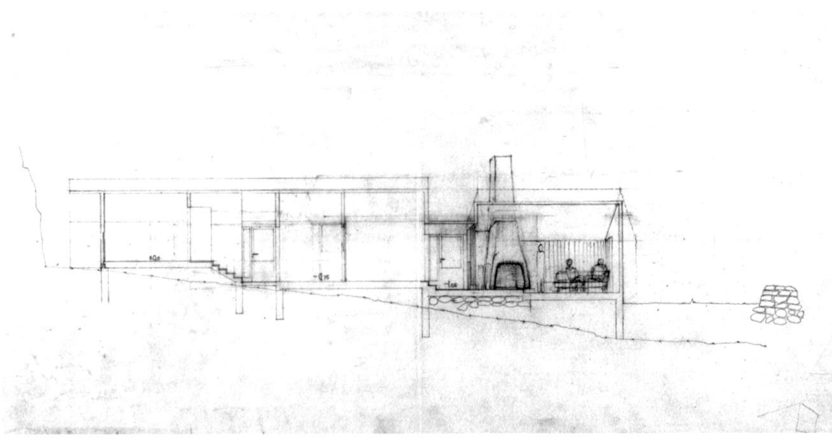

FIGURE 6.15 Preliminary section, Stennäs, Asplund, 1936

Source: The Swedish Center for Architecture and Design, ARKM.1988-02-10209

For those who might be aware that the stepping-stone closest to the entrance comes from the Woodland Cemetery, it is possible to read this contrast between vulnerable wood and immutable stone as a commentary on mortality. Despite the intention to identify the house with a timeless landscape, Asplund acknowledges that this structure, like a body, is all too perishable. Rather than using the pretense

FIGURE 6.16 View of entrance porch at Stennäs, Asplund, 1936–38

Source: Author photo

of longevity that comes with stone, as found in many Wright houses, Asplund prefers to draw attention to tragic irony in the manner of Strindberg or Nietzsche: as much as he may display a passionate identification with landscape, he reminds us of separateness, made clear by the white color, and mortality, by virtue of the easily rotting wood.

This interest in calculated ambiguity, familiar from earlier projects, also informs interior decisions. Beginning at the entrance at Stennäs, Asplund uses familiar devices to give clues about how the visitor might respond to the interior. The *Angel of Death* at Woodland Chapel and the door handles at the Stadsbibliotek come to mind as other examples of entrance gestures. There is no sculpture in this case, but there are several aspects that are telling. As you enter, you step on a broad, flat stone from the Woodland Cemetery. This abuts black-painted decking material of very narrow boards that turns to the vertical plane to meet the ground (see Figure 6.16). Meanwhile, the underside of the roof of the shallow entrance porch is painted deep red, the traditional color of Swedish farmhouses. Although no firm conclusions can be made, it is still possible to imagine that the red color is meant to encourage the visitor to study how the interior might relate to familiar old houses. The black decking material and black floor inside are more opaque gestures. While a Functionalist would want a reflective surface to reflect light, Asplund appears to be more interested in continuity with the stone surface, suggesting that one might imagine that the floor is, in fact, stone.

The other provocative statement at an entrance lies on the east side, where there is a small wooden staircase. Jones speculates that this could be a remnant of the original three-part scheme with open-air transitions between the parts (Jones 2006, 200). In any case, it does provide necessary access to the eastern side of the property. In a very late design-development drawing, the stair is shown with an undulating railing (Figure 6.17). This curved design for the stair was later abandoned in favor of a straight one where the profile of the treads and risers reads on the outside face of the railing with extended pieces of the floor, treads, and risers (Figure 6.18). It is noteworthy that the stair runs towards the south, corresponding to the slope of the land. Given the abandoned undulating scheme and the alignment of slope and run, it is possible to speculate that Asplund wished to relate this stair to the brick stair and swelling fireplace inside. This intention would be very much in keeping with his aforementioned tendency to provide clues at entrances to suggest possible interpretations of the interior.

However interesting, this entrance is just one of many entrances at Stennäs. The main entrance lies on the west side very close to where the tail meets the head, so to speak (see Figure 6.17). You enter at the level of the dining room, just above the stairs that descend to the living room. Immediately in front of you is a closet, made from closely spaced vertical pieces of bamboo that end two to three feet from the ceiling. It has the aspect of a semi-transparent phone booth and serves to create a transitional space before one enters the living room. Most wall and ceiling surfaces on the house are made from closely spaced white-painted

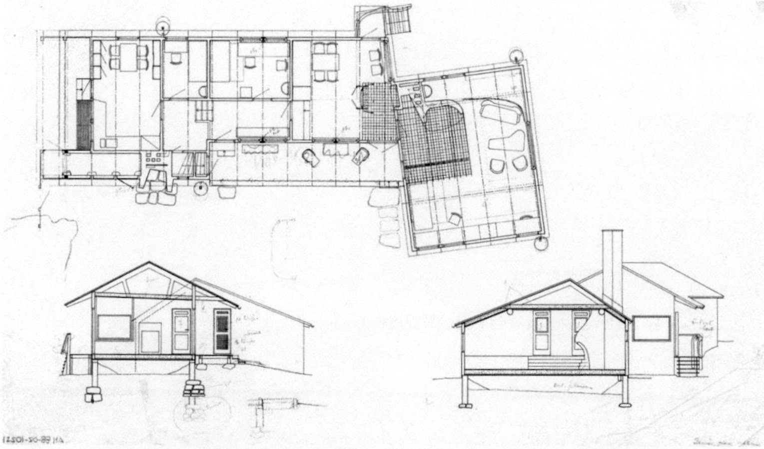

FIGURE 6.17 Final plan and sections, Stennäs, Asplund, circa 1937

Source: The Swedish Center for Architecture and Design, ARKM.1988-02-10251

boards, approximately five inches wide. Care has been taken to leave the joints open so there is a barely readable texture in the white surface.

The dining room, immediately ahead, has a built-in bench with a datum of rice paper that defines the back and small-diameter pieces of bamboo that close the area under the seat. The table, with white-painted chairs by Asplund, is arranged so the axis aligns with a large south-facing window where you view the inlet and the datum of the horizon. To the left from the dining room are a small bedroom and a bathroom on one level, followed by a kitchen with a small dining area on the next (see Figure 6.17). The long hallway is used for storage of chairs, hanging space for clothes, bookcases, and a chest of drawers. Additional space for sleeping can be found in a small cabin in the woods to the south of the entrance path.

Windows on all of these levels are primarily associated with furniture and calculated views. In other words, they are intended to relate to people sitting down for leisure, study, or dining. Though these places are visually connected to some parts of the landscape, there is no intention to break down all barriers between inside and outside. Asplund does not offer a panoramic view or general ambient daylighting, though on the east and west sides there are pairs of square windows. Instead, the experience of the outside is framed as an event, while the experience of the inside is preserved as a uniquely different experience. It is clear that Asplund did not want the interior to act as a substitute for exterior experience; although different parts of the house are related to reference points in the landscape, he preferred that his guests inhabit the outdoors to fully enjoy it. The ultimate experience, architectural or otherwise, was reserved for the top of the outcrop.

From the dining room, you descend down brick stairs to a large living room with an asymmetrical ceiling and a large picture window that frames a view of the inlet. At the east side of the room there is a desk next to a tall cabinet, while on

FIGURE 6.18 View of eastern stair at Stennäs, Asplund, 1936–38

Source: Author photo

the west side there is a long counter for workspace and three windows. The most extraordinary aspect of the living room, however, is the fireplace. Unlike Asplund's public buildings in this study, which feature a lofty room with a ceiling that evokes the sky, there is no such space here. Instead, to the right of the entry point and dining room there is an unusual episode where brick stairs extend into a mouth-like fireplace on the left and become the hearth (Figure 6.19). Unlike a Wright house, where fireplace and hearth represent the rock of stability, this fireplace and hearth are notably awkward and disconcerting. As Jones notes, old farmhouses frequently had large corner fireplaces made of white plaster on masonry, of which the Oktorp farmhouse at Skansen has an excellent example (Figure 6.20) (2006, 200). This fireplace, though white and built in the same manner, is a swelling rounded form that is large enough to sit within, as an assistant of Asplund's noted (198). Again, as at Observatorielunden, there is no tidy answer to this riddle. One is left to construct meanings from the themes of "body," "fire," and "stair." The aforementioned east entrance suggests an interpretation where the brick stair is accepted as an abstraction of landscape. If this is the case, the fireplace could be understood as a "body" that accommodates a "landscape," just as the rooms of the house climb up the slope. The fire, the part that unites them both, could be seen as the common source of vitality or the *élan vital*, to borrow Bergson's term.

The furniture, likewise, is both strange and familiar. Asplund designed a table, settee, and two armchairs for the area in front of the window (Figure 6.21). Of these, the table is the strangest of all. Like the fireplace, it appears to be a natural thing; the legs taper up from the floor in the manner of tree trunks. The tabletop, meanwhile, is curved on one side is to allow people to move easily around it. The settee and chairs are all upholstered above, with a white-painted structural frame exposed below, seeming both modern and traditional. The profile of the settee, however, is shaped like the wings of a butterfly or an exaggerated profile of a Victorian sofa, occupying an ambiguous zone between Nature and culture.

To locate this ambiguous area, Asplund depended on an intimate knowledge of vernacular forms on the part of visitors. He did not rely exclusively on vernacular form because his more important reference concerns vernacular site planning. The most distinctive quality of the Swedish farmhouse is the courtyard, a trait that persisted for centuries. This was a space of arrival and protection from wind and snow, bounded by barns and a very modest dwelling. Examples from the south in the region of Skåne are closed courts, while those from the north tend to be more open, with inventive responses to landscape (Figures 6.22 and 6.23) (Carlsson 1912, 10). Many examples also show how low walls of fieldstone also contribute to spatial definition (Figure 6.24). At Stennäs, a courtyard is conjured from the edge of the outcrop and a stone wall (see Figure 6.2). For some visitors at Stennäs, this would not be recognizable as a traditional courtyard. It is worth bearing in mind, however, the housing project at Södermalm and the site plan of the Stockholm Exhibition, where natural features (outcrops, water, and groves) are used to complete the definition of a space that is at once both cultural and natural. At Stennäs, this balance in possible readings has been adjusted to the point where

FIGURE 6.19
Interior view of fireplace and steps in living room at Stennäs, Asplund, 1936–38

Source: Sune Sundahl photo, The Swedish Center for Architecture and Design, ARKM. 1985-109-035

FIGURE 6.20
Interior view of fireplace at Oktorpgården, Skansen, Stockholm, moved from Halland, eighteenth and nineteenth centuries

Source: Nordic Museum, NMA.0045005

FIGURE 6.21
Interior view of living room looking south, Stennäs, Asplund, 1936–38

Source: Andreas Feininger photo, The Swedish Center for Architecture and Design, ARKM. 1962-101-1166

natural space, cultural space, and contemporary use overlap without one dominating presence. This delicate integration of the vernacular and landscape is Asplund's most extraordinary gift and distinguishes this house from a demonstration of Functionalism.

His Swedish contemporaries, the fellow authors of *acceptera* and others, preferred to see vernacular buildings as models of Functionalist thinking.[3] In this vein, a true Functionalist, when designing a summerhouse, would give priority to light, ventilation, views, and patios. At Stennäs, Asplund gives a very different account of function, where the vernacular is not used as a model of Functionalism. Instead it is referenced for its phenomenological qualities; in particular, he is concerned how these buildings might reveal or relate to the landscape or the body. As mentioned earlier, some National Romantic painters presented traditional buildings in this way. In many cases, these qualities of old buildings were a matter of intuition or an indirect outcome of a functional agenda. In many respects, Asplund reverses these priorities: functions are found within a larger agenda of calculated poetic relationships with the existing landscape.

Asplund was not alone in taking an interest in the vernacular in the late 1930s. Jones mentions Hugo Häring, Le Corbusier, Aalto, and Wright, among others, who shared this preoccupation (Jones 2006, 200). All of these architects engaged different traditions on very different terms. In some instances, the reference did not go beyond materiality, while others used "organic" architectural ideas both to satisfy functional needs and to relate to landscape. For Häring, vernacular design was marked by the stigma of Nazi ideology. While the vernacular certainly had nationalist meanings in Sweden, it did not bear the stigma of any particular ideology, though left-leaning Functionalists tried to claim its ancestry. What distinguishes Asplund in this company is his relative restraint. He wanted active relationships with landscape, but he also wanted a vernacular ancestry to be discernible. "Organic" gestures, as one finds at the fireplace, were calculated to have multiple readings, including the body, the vernacular, and pure invention in the manner of Scharoun or Aalto.

It is fair to ask in this context why he wished the visitor to regard vernacular design as closely related to landscape and the qualities of the body. One answer is that Swedes sought identity in all three directions—the natural world, the cultural world, and the qualities of the body. For some, this list would have also included Functionalism as a confident claim to the possibilities of the future. It is important to remember, however, that there were (and perhaps are) no strict boundaries between culture and the natural world. For many Swedes, culture is indistinguishable from landscape; skerries, juniper, lingonberries, *and* old farmhouses are all treasured parts of national identity. While Southern Europeans made, and still make, careful distinctions between wild and domestic landscapes (Descola 2013, 48–56), no such boundaries exist in Sweden. What foreigners would understand as wild places, such as forests, outcrops, and skerries, were always considered as human habitat.

4. PLANSKISS AF GÅRD VID ARLÖF.

FIGURE 6.22 Skåne farmstead plan

Source: Gustaf Carlsson, *Gamla Svenska Allmogehem*, Stockholm: A. B. Hasse W. Tullberg, 1912

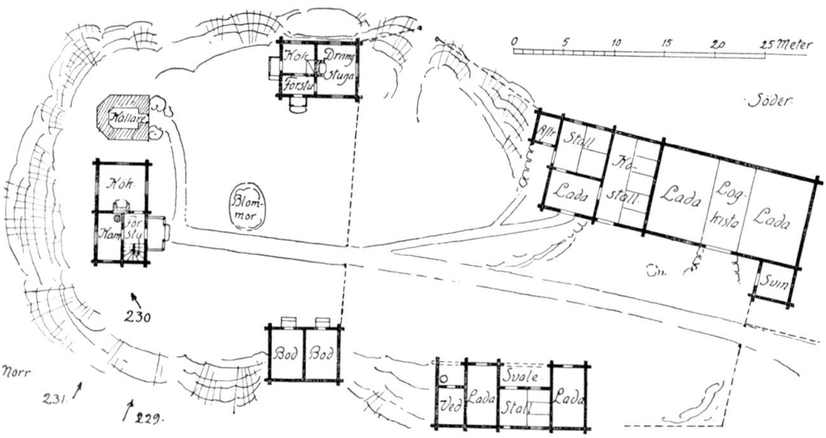

232. PLAN AF BERGLUNDS I SLÄDEKÄRR.

FIGURE 6.23 Dalsland farmstead plan

Source: Gustaf Carlsson, *Gamla Svenska Allmogehem*, Stockholm: A. B. Hasse W. Tullberg, 1912

FIGURE 6.24 Halland farm stone wall

Source: Gustaf Carlsson, *Gamla Svenska Allmogehem*, Stockholm: A. B. Hasse W. Tullberg, 1912

This may help to explain why Asplund sought to use landscape architecture and architecture as an art object that functions to bring culture and landscape together in one image. This is in contrast with the art object that serves to imaginatively transcend the known world or the triumph of formalism (Lofthouse 2005, 28–38). According to Asplund's version, the vernacular is not there for sentimental purposes. Instead, it is contributing a view through time such that the present is viewed as an outgrowth of old beliefs and practices.[4] The mound with Meditation Grove at the Woodland Cemetery, for example, is designed to be seen as a sculpted body part, an archaic burial place, and a place of reflection. According to this thinking, one can assume that Asplund felt that our consciousness should never completely reside in the present; we should rather inhabit a place where past, present, and future overlap and embrace what George Kubler would call "the reality of duration" (Kubler 1962, 124).

Another version of a concept of time is T. S. Eliot's thinking about "the historical sense." This sensitivity, in his account, is "a perception not only of the pastness of the past, but of its presence" and "a sense of the timeless as well as the temporal and of the timeless and temporal together" (Eliot 1964, 49). A work of art that is invested with this sense, he explains, has the capacity to compel a reinterpretation of artworks that came before (40). For example, those who have seen the bulging fireplace at Stennäs could find it difficult to ever look upon traditional Swedish fireplaces in the same way again. This phenomenon can also work between media. If you had occasion to look down on a Swedish farmhouse next to the sea after viewing Nordström's *The Neighboring Farm* (see Figure 3.6), you might have a sharper sense of how a ridgeline can relate to skerries and the horizon beyond.

In Asplund's case, what frequently forces this reconsideration of the past are his references to the human body and other gestures, which give the illusion that all parts are invested with life. This pertains directly to Vitalism, a recurrent theme in Asplund's work since the beginning of his career. As mentioned earlier, Vitalism as a philosophical topic has ancient origins dating back to Aristotle. Many asked at the time whether life resides in mechanism or whether life animates mechanism. The topic took on new perspectives in the late nineteenth and early twentieth centuries, penetrating into painting, drama, science, philosophy, and theology.

Nietzsche's *The Birth of Tragedy* was a primary source of inspiration for this diverse cultural movement. He wished to draw attention to the critical importance of the chorus in early Greek drama, in particular the plays of Aeschylus. Here, there was a balance or reconciliation between a cerebral detached perspective, which he calls Apollonian, and a Dionysian response, derived from the body and the senses, represented by music and dance. Later Greek plays, at the time of Euripides, came under the influence of Socrates and lost the vital qualities of the chorus and the Dionysian response. Socrates, Nietzsche claims, was later enshrined as the paragon of scientific thinking in more modern times. This led to a dead end in scientific thinking, when any gifted thinker "finds himself staring into impenetrable darkness" (Nietzsche 2000, 84). If he sees at this time how "logic curls around itself and finally bites its own tail—then the new form of knowledge breaks through, *tragic knowledge*, which in order to be tolerated, needs art as a protection and remedy" (84).

This appeal to the necessity for art and the essential qualities of the body found a receptive audience among painters, sculptors, writers, and dramatists. Though labeled as Vitalism, this was never an organized movement and had innumerable branches, mainly in Scandinavia and Northern Europe.[5] Some artists, for example, identified the values of Vitalism with ancient Greece. A group in Denmark took this to an extreme by launching a short-lived art colony called the Refsnaes Hellene Community, where Greek dress and Spartan living were required (Oelsner 2011, 163). These artists, among others, placed great emphasis on restoring bonds between culture and the natural world. "Culture, after a period of decline, was to be saved by a cultivation of life 'close to nature' and natural hygiene practices; while the landscape itself, with its cyclically unfolding seasons, could be understood as a framework for cultural rebirth" (159). Other offshoots of this branch of Vitalism included naturism, which became widespread at the turn of the century, and the Olympic movement.

The other main current of Vitalism was scientific in origin and oriented towards proving the existence of a unity between organic and inorganic matter. Though many espoused this cause, one of the leaders was Ernst Haeckel, a professor at the University of Jena. In his book *The Riddle of the Universe*, he presents the doctrine of Monism, where the central tenet is the "law of substance." "The two fundamental forms of substance, ponderable matter and ether, are not dead and only moved by extrinsic force, but they are endowed with sensation and will (though naturally of the lowest grade); they experience an inclination for condensation, a dislike of strain; they strive after the one and struggle against the other" (Haeckel 1900, 220).

Though he makes no attempt to argue that this is a mark of divine creation, he makes it clear that this design of the universe is a source of beauty and worthy of reverence. He writes that "the astonishment with which we gaze upon the starry heavens and the microscopic life in a drop of water, the awe with which we trace the remarkable working of energy in the motion of matter, the reverence with which we grasp the universal dominance of the law of substance throughout the universe—all these are part of our emotional life, falling under the heading of 'natural religion'" (344).

One of the links between the scientific and artistic variations of Vitalism was August Strindberg, the Swedish dramatist, who freely engaged in painting and scientific experiments at different times in his life. His paintings were guided by a spontaneous method where he would arrive at a subject, mainly landscapes, in the process of painting. Even after the painting was completed, he could find new interpretations, according to his "frame of mind." Despite these diverse responses, there was still a clear difference between them. "Every picture," he explained, "is double bottomed, as it were: each has an exoteric aspect that everyone can make out, albeit with a little effort, and an esoteric one for the painter and a chosen few" (Hedström 2001, 48). His scientific experiments, meanwhile, were dedicated to proving a link between the organic and inorganic. He approached this with mystical devotion; at one point he wrote, "rock is living and can bring forth life through fermentation. Coal is born of the mountain" (Feuk 2001, 118). He translates this phenomenon in a literary way in a story called "The Stone Man," about a convict who works on a rocky hillside. When he and his fellow convicts apply silt dredged from a harbor to the hill, it changes into a green landscape. The hill is transformed from the inorganic to the organic, thereby also restoring the convict's spirit and faith in his fellow man (Strindberg 1928, 49–60).

The other dimension of Strindberg's art, besides his life as a dramatist, was concerned with Swedish culture and landscape, particularly the Stockholm archipelago. "It was a landscape that matched his temperament, a juxtaposition of 'the brooding and the smiling, the lean and the rich, the domestic and the wild' " (Vowles 1965, xii). In his *Sverige Natur* of 1900, he made characteristic geological diagrams of the coastline of the archipelago that his collaborator transformed into etchings (Hedström 2001, 23). Previously, in 1887, he had written *The Natives of Hemsö*, about a small group of fishermen and farmers in the archipelago. The main character, a scheming mainlander named Carlsson, climbs to a high point to admire the landscape when making a critical decision. Though he is just a farmhand, he is overcome by the sensual beauty of water, woods, fields and red farmhouses in the light of the setting sun (Strindberg 1965, 82). It is worth noting the role of landscape as a source of guidance for a farmer and the ease with which the farmhouses become part of the natural scene. Carlsson, alas, makes the wrong decisions and is later consumed by a blizzard as symbolic revenge for his participation in demolishing a small island for possible minerals.

Despite the advent of formalist modern art and Functionalism in Sweden, Strindberg's brand of Vitalism continued to have an afterlife in the realm of poetry. Among the most celebrated poets at the time that Stennäs was built were those who contributed to an anthology published in 1929 called *Fem Unga* or *Five Young Ones*, namely Erik Asklund, Josef Kjellgren, Artur Lundkvist, Harry Martinson, and Gustav Sandgren. Of these, Harry Martinson had the most enduring career, particularly as an essayist and poet of Nature. His description of how the natural world and the life of the mind might come together portrays another way to understand Vitalism in twentieth-century Sweden. In *Views from a Tuft of Grass*, he acknowledges the difficulty of exactly describing a poetic response to the natural world but insists that it is an everyday phenomenon and common to all of us.

> The description of nature as a literary art occurs in a realm that can never be fully and completely caught with words, or grasped with any maneuver of the imagination. But it is everyone's great, outdoor background to life, and to work with it is to be directly at one with both the profoundest and airiest aspects of life. Thus reality and magic are in one and the same image: the nature of reality, the nature that exists, simultaneously flowering in the

> imagination and tangible in the harsh grove of always. In that expression itself—the nature of reality—the mystery of reality is suggested. In order to find it, you have only to experience how your habitual way of seeing sometimes can be altered into a visionary way of seeing; you discover that the nature of reality resounds the way a sense of foreboding surges out of the things themselves.
>
> (Martinson 2005, 15–16)[6]

It is noteworthy that Martinson's description of "a visionary way of seeing" involves more than an experience of delight. It also appears to be marked by a glimpse of eternity and a heightened sense of mortality, two themes that are apparent in Asplund's work.

The persistence of Vitalism in Scandinavia supports the claim of Lofthouse that there are two sources of modernism in the nineteenth century. Though both may have been inspired by Nietzsche, the more well-known branch descends from the development of abstraction in France and the rebellion against the Academy, while Vitalism spread in Protestant countries of Northern Europe, where earlier Romantic painters had established a culture of nature worship (Rosenblum 1975). "The formalist narrative of the rise of modern art may be read as mimicking the Apollonian trajectory, roughly conceived—that is to say, the route of formal values, transcendence and abstraction—leaving the Vitalist, Dionysian alternative to nurture 'immanence' and 'realism'" (Lofthouse 2005, 32). Unlike artists, such as those championed by Clement Greenberg, who found spiritual value in the transcendent qualities of abstraction, Vitalist artists "sought out the spiritual in life and things, almost like a radicalized and often perverse doctrine of incarnation" (36).

This background is intended to suggest that Functionalism did not divert Asplund from a Vitalist agenda. There is no evidence that he read Ernst Haeckel, or Nietzsche, but he was a devotee of Strindberg.[7] In any case, all three were part of a prevailing discourse in the early part of the century, when Asplund was finding himself as a person and an architect. If Stennäs is seen as a Vitalist creation, the landscape and house are very much a Dionysian phenomenon, following Nietzsche's formula. The house associates itself with the outcrop, receives the landscape to the west, and contorts to respond to the view of the inlet. It makes no pretense that there is a cerebral order that exists apart from the landscape, as one finds at the Stadsbibliotek, or that it has any durability to rival that of stone. Similarly, there is no attempt to associate machines with landscape, an agenda that was expressed forcefully at the Stockholm Exhibition.

It is appropriate to ask, however, what messages Asplund's Vitalist agenda might carry. Using his works and intellectual milieu as a guide, one can provide some speculative answers. First, he would wish the user to know that body and mind belong together, where body is the entrée to the natural world and the life of the senses; this is one essential message that is enhanced, nuanced, and edited over time. Among his projects, Stadsbiblioteket and Observatorielunden stand out as the clearest expression of this intention. Second, he would add a reassurance that body and mind belong together *in* a characteristic Swedish landscape, be it pine forest, outcrops, or skerries. This is not a familiar form of nationalism that is known through conformity but is rather reached through an individual's own reconciliation of mind, body, landscape, and culture. Finally, as the landscape and house at Stennäs suggest, poetic experience, through the agency of art, is the only means to arrive at this reconciliation.

Notes

1 The top of a skerry is also the preferred retreat for contemplation of Axel Borg, the hero in Strindberg's novel *By the Open Sea* (1890).
2 The wood columns at the porch of Woodland Chapel that meet the stone floor are equally impractical.
3 This argument was made by Gustaf Näsström in *Svensk funktionalism* (Stockholm, Sweden: Bokförlaget Natur och kultur, 1930).
4 Strindberg expresses a similar sentiment in his preface to *Miss Julie*, explaining how his "souls (characters) are conglomerates of past and present stages of culture." See August Strindberg, *Miss Julie and Other Plays* (Oxford: Oxford University Press, 1998), 60.
5 As previously mentioned, Stuart Wrede draws attention to a source of inspiration for this movement in Romantic painters of Northern Europe in the early nineteenth century. See Stuart Wrede, "The Garden in the Anthropocene Era," in *The Garden of Life*, ed. Karin Sidén (Stockholm, Sweden: Prins Eugens Waldemarsudde, 2014).
6 This excerpt from *Views of a Tuft of Grass* by Harry Martinson, translated by Erland Anderson and Lars Nordström, is reprinted with the permission of The Permissions Company, Inc. on behalf of Green Integer, www.greeninteger.com.
7 See Stuart Wrede, *The Architecture of Erik Gunnar Asplund* (Cambridge, MA: MIT Press, 1980), 24–25, 54.

References

Andersson, Thorbjörn. 1998. "The Functionalism of the Gardening Art." In *Sweden: Twentieth Century Architecture*, edited by Claes Caldenby, Jöran Lindvall, and Wilfred Wang, 226–24. Munich, Germany: Prestel.

Carlsson, Gustaf. 1912. *Gamla Svenska Allmogehem*. 2 vols. Stockholm, Sweden: A. B. Hasse and W. Tullberg.

Descola, Philippe. 2013. *Beyond Nature and Culture*. Chicago, IL: University of Chicago Press.

Eliot, T. S. 1964. *The Sacred Wood: Essays on Poetry and Criticism*. London: Methuen.

Feuk, Douglas. 2001. "Dreaming Materialized." In *Strindberg: Painter and* Photographer, edited by Per Hedström, 117–30. New Haven, CT: Yale University Press.

Haeckel, Ernst. 1900. *The Riddle of the Universe*. New York: Harper and Bros.

Hedenstierna, Bengt. 1960. *Geographical Features of Stockholms Skärgård*. International Geographical Congress.

Hedström, Per. 2001. "Strindberg as a Pictorial Artist—a Survey." In *Strindberg: Painter and Photographer*, edited by Per Hedström. 9–102. New Haven, CT: Yale University Press.

Jones, Peter Blundell. 2006. *Gunnar Asplund*. London: Phaidon Press.

Kubler, George. 1962. *The Shape of Time*. New Haven, CT: Yale University Press.

Lofthouse, Richard. 2005. *Vitalism in Modern Art, c. 1900–1950*. Lewiston, NY: Edwin Mellen Press.

Martinson, Harry. 2005. *Views from a Tuft of Grass*. Translated by Erland Anderson and Lars Nordström. Copenhagen, Denmark: Green Integer.

Nietzsche, Friedrich. 2000. *The Birth of Tragedy*. Oxford: Oxford University Press.

Oelsner, Gertrud. 2011. "Healthy Nature." In *The Spirit of Vitalism: Health, Beauty and Strength in Danish Art, 1890–1940*, edited by Gertrud Oelsner and Gertrud Hvidberg-Hansen, 158–97. Copenhagen, Denmark: Museum Tusculanum Press.

Rosenblum, Robert. 1975. *Modern Painting and the Northern Romantic Tradition: Friedrich to Rothko*. New York: Harper and Row.

Rudberg, Eva. 1998. "Early Functionalism, 1930–1940." In *Sweden: Twentieth Century Architecture*, edited by Claes Caldenby, Jöran Lindvall, and Wildfred Wang, 80–109. Munich, Germany: Prestel.

Strindberg, August. 1928. "The Stone Man." In *Sweden's Best Stories*, edited by Hanna Larsen, 49–60. New York: W. W. Norton.

——. 1965. *The Natives of Hemsö*. New York: Paul S. Erikson.

Vowles, Richard. 1965. Introduction to *The Natives of Hemsö*. New York: Paul S. Erikson.

7
CONCLUSION

The Woodland Cemetery initiates a way of thinking where an idea about a site precedes an architectural idea. Asplund's strategies related to this approach evolved over thirty years. Even the advent of Functionalism does not present a complete break; it is simply a more expressive palette to achieve his aims. He believed in the urgency of the housing crisis and the importance of expressing the modern era, but, as he likely wrote in *acceptera*, he did not wish to advocate for comfort and utility "at the expense of spiritual values" (Åhrén et al. 2008, 234). Though he went to some trouble to define tradition in the modern era as a defense of "straightforwardness, moderation and friendliness" (315), he did not give equal attention to spelling out "spiritual values."

His major projects, however, make the case that these values belong to landscape. As many National Romantic painters demonstrated, it has a counterpart for the full range of human emotion, both exalted states and mundane ones, and it can clearly define the domain of communal life and that of the individual. Given this potential, Asplund's aim was to prompt the imagination to make the poetic exchange between building and landscape. This can involve an association between seemingly dissimilar elements, like an airplane and a perennial garden. It can also exploit layers of cultural meaning that originate in landscape and permit a vision of time to the remote past. On a fundamental level, it can simply invite comparison between an interior architectural sequence and one found in the landscape. A building, in these cases, is a secondary constructed landscape that can take advantage of this fundamental connection between the mind and the natural world. Though superficially simple, this insight prompted a collection of complex design ideas that can be roughly classified as concepts. Because the boundaries between these concepts are often blurred, any description of them is inherently imprecise; one particular design idea has the capacity to exist as two concepts at once.

Outside to inside. The preeminent concept among all those that follow, this is where one brings a significant experience of the *outside* to the *inside*, followed by a possibly different response to the outside. For example, after taking in the sculpted landscape and Meditation Grove at the North Entry of the Woodland Cemetery, one might enter the Chapel of the Holy Cross and imaginatively transpose the peristyle that lies within to the landscape outside, or vice versa. In a similar vein, one might climb the hill called Observatoriekullen after viewing the Stadsbibliotek rotunda and see the panoramic view of Stockholm as a compendium of knowledge. Alternatively, one can climb the hill first and perhaps then see the library's rotunda as an embodiment of the Cosmos. The implied intention is to prompt one to draw upon immediate memories and encourage a poetic exchange between architectural space and the natural world. While this preoccupation is characteristic of much of Asplund's work, it was also shared by Ivar Tengbom, another practitioner of Neoclassicism in Stockholm.

Layered meanings. A reoccurring concept is the layering of meanings within a landscape. In the case of the landscape around the Woodland Chapel, this may pertain to the origins of belief, as it is both a churchyard and a sacred grove. At Stockholm Exhibition's Ellida Restaurant this device can have a hallucinogenic quality when a forest becomes both a building and a ship. It can also assume a Functionalist guise when the terraced Festplats at the exhibition becomes both a concert venue and a garden by virtue of waist-high flower boxes. In another example, the layers document actual or imagined history in the courtyard at Stennäs; it is simultaneously a meadow at the base of a cliff, a farmyard, and a pleasure ground. These layers help to encourage an inclusive and non-ideological view of the world. They also promote a poetic pleasure in the unfolding of meanings and the appreciation of their coexistence. Finally, their simultaneous presence can induce a vision of time into the remote past, an agenda that was shared by German philologists and Swedish Neoclassical architects.

Parallel sequences and reciprocal spaces. A landscape sequence of places will be placed side by side with an architectural one. For example, the passage from the reflecting pool to hilltop at Observatorielunden is the companion to the sequence from sidewalk to rotunda at the Stadsbibliotek. Likewise, the sequence from outcrop to meadow to salt marsh has a counterpart in the terraced section of the house at Stennäs. A related concept is reciprocal spaces, where two places, though quite different, are positioned so that one might be surveyed or recalled from the other. The Meditation Grove and the Monument Hall at the Woodland Cemetery are notable in this respect. The Chapel of the Holy Cross and the Hill of Repose are also counterparts, though without direct visual contact. Both parallel sequences and reciprocal spaces can be seen as devices to assist the poetic exchange mentioned earlier between inside and outside.

Framed landscape. What would normally be considered as wild or untouched landscape is framed by the nearby presence of architecture or other means in order to be understood with new significance. The forest around the Woodland Chapel is bounded by the wall of a churchyard to assume an enhanced reading as a sacred place. Also, by virtue of its proximity to the court below, the wild plants amid the rocks at the top of the outcrop at Stennäs take on the character of a found garden. This concept is closely related to the landscape approach of Hermelin, a distinguished landscape architect of the first half of the twentieth century. According to his thesis, the landscape architect's job in Sweden was "more a matter of carefully integrating the building into the existing landscape" (Andersson 1997, 283). It can also be put into the context of Rutger Sernander, a professor of biology who campaigned for a new kind of park in the twenties that would preserve rough outcrops and groves of old trees.[1]

Spatial collaboration. As a related concept, Asplund also uses architecture in collaboration with landscape features to define and enclose outdoor spaces. At the housing project at Södermalm, an outcrop forms one end of a small piazza. A grove of trees and a lagoon make two sides of the Festplats at the Stockholm Exhibition. Lastly, the outcrop at Stennäs serves as the north edge of a courtyard at the entrance. Again, this concept assists in creating the aforementioned poetic phenomena where landscape can be imagined as architecture or architecture can be viewed as landscape. Likewise, as related above, the shared space can alternate between court and meadow. This transposition between architecture and landscape also occurs in National Romantic painting and architecture.

Art of arrival. In all projects under study here, works of art or ambiguous gestures are made at entrances to buildings or landscapes. In some cases, these can be seen as part of a rhetoric of inclusiveness to reassure visitors with different beliefs. The crucifix and Meditation Grove at the North Entry of the Woodland Cemetery, for example, perform this function, among others. Artworks of arrival can also actively support the interpretation of a landscape. The *Angel of Death* at the Woodland Chapel, for example, is both Christian and pre-Christian, analogous to the manner in which the chapel's churchyard defines a sacred grove. Finally, there is an instance where the "art of arrival" engages objects, architecture, *and* landscape. This tripartite phenomenon existed at the Stockholm Exhibition, where the Transportation Building embraced an airplane and boats that faced the Alnarp garden opposite. In all of these cases, Asplund invites the visitor to either see what they wish or do the more difficult work of reconciling different elements. The second option allows far deeper insight into larger motivations once the visitor is completely familiar with both landscape and building.

The high point. Every project has a high point or place of contemplation where a work of architecture can be understood as part of a landscape or vice versa. In some cases, this is a natural formation such as Observatoriekullen, which looks down on the Stadsbibliotek, and the top of the outcrop at his summerhouse at Stennäs, which commands a view of the house and the harbor beyond. In another instance, the high point is a constructed landscape, such as Sigurd Lewerentz's Meditation Grove, which overlooks the Woodland Crematorium. In addition, this purpose was served architecturally by the press box that surveyed the Festplats at the Stockholm Exhibition. As in Strindberg's description of Stockholm from a hill at the opening of *The Red Room*,[2] the individual is put in a position of power to overlook the building below, observing mundane activities as well as the grandeur of the sky and the horizon. From this vantage point, functioning like the art of arrival, the visitor is invited to construct multiple associations between all the elements within view. In particular, the high point serves as a prompt to contemplate the communal life that exists below.

View to the outside. This same interest in the simultaneous appreciation of all views, both sublime and intimate, is present in some of Asplund's buildings. These have interior spaces that invoke the illusion of the sky or the Cosmos while also maintaining a view corridor to the natural world. At the Woodland Chapel, for example, the door was to be left open to maintain a view of the forest from within. At the Woodland Crematorium, the curtain wall at the Chapel of the Holy Cross was designed and built to be retractable to permit a view of the open landscape. Finally, at the Stadsbibliotek, there is a drinking fountain in the south reading room, overlooking Observatorielunden, that takes the shape of the reflecting pool. This calculated view to the outside suggests the necessity of a release from the abstracted reality of an interior and a reminder of the landscape that was seen on arrival.

Diagonal perspectives. An oblique view, either from a building or towards a building, gathers foreground, middle ground, and background into a unique relationship. This is the essential idea that Piper learned at Stourhead and applied to great effect at Drottningholm Palace Garden and Haga Park, linking open space and multiple pavilions. In contrast to familiar Beaux Arts planning, it is non-hierarchical; a building is not cast in a dominant role, as an axial view would suggest. Instead, buildings are more often seen to advantage in three dimensions, rather than in elevation. While carefully planned by Asplund in perspectives, these views allow a spontaneous discovery by the visitor, as one would experience in the natural world. Photographs confirm these deliberate perspectives, including looking across the reflecting pool at the obscured Stadsbibliotek, admiring the Advertising Mast and Paradise Restaurant across the flower boxes of the Festplats, and appreciating the Transportation Building from the Alnarp garden. The most celebrated of all is the view from the Monument Hall at the Woodland Cemetery, across a small reflecting pool, towards the Hill of Repose and the Meditation Grove.

In the introduction, reference was made to the essential tension within the Swedish cultural agenda in the early twentieth century. On one hand, there was a commitment to become a modern state. On the other, there was an unwillingness to abandon deep-seated values and traditions. National Romanticism could certainly address the latter impulse but had little capacity to treat the former. The major public projects of Asplund's career were ideal for addressing this dilemma; he had the challenge of treating death, self-advancement, and a progressive vision of the future. All of these programs embraced strong emotions, including grief, ambition, and hope. His inclination to search for heterogeneous solutions, where archaic, historical, and progressive agendas could converge, served him well in this task. Strindberg wrote, "My souls (characters) are conglomerates of past and present stages of culture, bits out of books and newspapers, scraps of humanity, torn shreds of once fine clothing now turned to rags, exactly as the human soul is stitched together" (Strindberg 1998, 60).

Either through intuition or conscious reflection, Asplund discovered that landscape was the ideal medium to create this composite portrait. It is by nature ambiguous; what is cultural easily overlaps with what is natural. In the context of Sweden in particular, it carries the cultural weight of prehistory; the natural world is not only delightful and miserable, a counterpart to daily life, it also speaks of their most distant origins. "The break in tradition caused by the advent of Christianity was not as great as might have been expected, and a number of conceptions of an ethereal landscape, formulated a couple thousand years ago, have accompanied us from heathen times right up to the present" (Andersson 1997, 281). Finally, as Sweden responded to the loss of Finland and Norway, the native landscape became the dwelling place of national feeling. Bearing this in mind, if it were possible for Swedes to see time in a landscape, they could also see themselves; Strindberg's dramatic conception could have a physical reality.

This status of landscape in Sweden allowed Neoclassicism to assume a unique significance that would not exist elsewhere. It had the capacity to give a new visual form to a conception of eternity that already existed in the landscape. This was made possible through the thinking of Nietzsche and those he influenced. In this way, the search for the qualities of the pre-Homeric could reveal alternative ways of thinking about culture in Sweden in the early twentieth century. This is done by introducing ideas of the sublime and "noncorporeal" within the agenda of National Romanticism. For example, though the Woodland Chapel may have the massing of a Norse house, in sympathy with National Romanticism, thanks to its interior dome, it becomes an expression about family, home, landscape, *and* the Cosmos. Landscape and family have been united with the eternal and boundless.

At the Woodland Chapel, landscape is a complement to an indoor experience. At the Stadsbibliotek, on the other hand, landscape becomes a parallel sequence to an architectural one. In this context, qualities of monumentality reside mutually in both landscape and architecture, each evoking eternity in their respective ways. This allows the visitor to imaginatively translate the qualities of one to the other, where the library is understood as landscape and vice versa. In this instance, landscape and architecture can enter into a phenomenal relationship where what is remembered is overlaid on what is seen.

With the advent of Functionalism in Asplund's work, the weight of monumentality is assumed by landscape almost exclusively. The Stockholm Exhibition demonstrates a new relationship where the massive Festplats, the grove of trees, and the shorefront assume the dominant position, while buildings derive their meanings from direct exposure to the outdoors. However, Asplund presents Functionalism here, in contrast to the diverse exotic pavilions at Drottningholm and Haga, as garden urbanism; light, ethereal structures make a townscape and relate their programs to gardens, a forest, open spaces, and water. The monumentality of the landscape is asserted even more forcefully at the North Entry of the Woodland Cemetery, where the crematorium, like the Stockholm Exhibition, is organized as a fragment of urbanism. Here, however, the Roman house becomes the subtext, another example of a hybrid. Asplund's own house at Stennäs is equally deferential to the landscape. In this case, however, monumentality is expressed by the adjoining cliff, a found landscape. The house and court, meanwhile, both take on an ambivalent character, somewhere between a meadow, a farmyard, and a patio.

In addition to this calculated ambiguity, it was Vitalism, or a poetic conceit that might animate landscape and architecture alike, that endowed the new monumental landscape with modernity. Through the force of imagination, he was able to reveal strange corporeal qualities in familiar features, including a sculpture of an angel, a mound of earth, a floating garden, and a farmhouse fireplace, among other elements. In this way, a visitor was given the possibility of imagining alternatives or conceiving thoughts that were not possible before. In a society that placed increasing emphasis on solidarity, thanks to Social Democratic dogma, this allowed space for individualism and national feeling to coexist. This kind of modernity, which derives from the philosophy of Nietzsche, is somewhat close to the aestheticism of Vilhelm Ekelund, who advocated the point of view of the artist, or the poetic perspective of Harry Martinson "in the harsh grove of always" (Martinson 2005, 15–16).

If Asplund had not died in 1940 at age fifty-five, we would have more examples of creative and ambiguous relationships between landscape and architecture. With the exception of his participation in the *acceptera* manifesto, he left only his landscapes and buildings, without any hard and fast doctrine. Although the Stockholm School of landscape design has an independent lineage, some traces of influence can be seen in the work of Erik Glemme, who was in charge of renovating Observatorielunden in the 1940s after a new subway line was excavated. The most specific example is seen at Tegnér Grove, where Glemme designed a meandering stream from the hilltop in the manner of Asplund's watercourse at Observatorielunden.

There were other Swedish architects from the middle of the century who took an interest in landscape relationships, either encouraged by Asplund's example or through cultural inclination. Sven Markelius's own house at Kvinge from 1945 beautifully frames a found garden (Andersson 1998, 227). Ralph Erskine demonstrates strong site relationships in his Tourist Hotel at Borgafjäll from 1948 as well as many housing projects over decades, including those at Ekerö (1985–90) and Sandviken (1973–78). Crematoria and cemeteries were built in forests in other parts of Sweden later in the twentieth century. Among the more successful was one at Gävle (1954) by Alf Engström, Gunnar Landberg, Bengt Larsson, and Alvar Törneman.

In the context of these examples, Asplund's achievement stands out for its nuance and thoughtfulness. Certainly, other architects have embraced both the design of landscapes and buildings, but few in the modern era have succeeded, let alone attempted, to consistently place landscape as a primary emphasis, while drawing upon ideas from painting, philosophy, and the dramatic arts.[3] Despite this distinction, Asplund has been admired over the years for other reasons. English architects of the fifties embraced him as a harbinger of the New Pragmatism in Swedish architecture. Later, in the seventies and eighties, postmodern architects appreciated him for his ease with references to the past and his skill at composing elevations.[4]

While this study intends to direct attention to a different aspect of Asplund's work, it should not be considered conclusive. The evidence cited lies within the work itself and the thought of the time. As part of their strength, however, these projects will always be subject to further interpretation. The intention has been to introduce avenues of further inquiry and to inspire contemporary practitioners. In particular, at this time when the certainties of the natural world are being undermined, the garden presents the most powerful tool to direct culture through poetic means. Bernard Lassus comments that "gardens have always foretold in advance the relationships between man and nature and between society and nature" (Bann 1998, 184).[5]

There is no doubt that Sweden is a special case in this respect. It is still possible, however, that a contemporary designer might learn lessons from Asplund's work, where landscapes play a dominant role and actively engage buildings. One would be a reminder that a landscape has a more powerful hold on emotions than a building and is far more legible to the uninitiated.[6] Another would concern the design of landscapes for introspection and how they might relate to seeing the past, all the way to the most archaic level. Finally, the greatest gift would come from landscapes that encourage a pleasure in ambiguity and show where imagination can find a home.

Notes

1 See Rutger Sernander, *Stockholms Natur* (Uppsala, Sweden: Almqvist & Wiksells Forläg, 1926).
2 Strindberg 2009, 9–20.
3 This is an enormous topic that requires considerable erudition. Some of those who should be mentioned include Vignola, Kent, Lutyens, and Wright. Several modern examples are covered by Caroline Constant in *The Modern Architectural Landscape* (Minneapolis, MN: University of Minnesota Press, 2012).
4 Colin St. John Wilson praised him for his skillful use of Neoclassicism to respond to context without the repressive intent of Albert Speer. See Colin St. John Wilson, "Gunnar Asplund and the Dilemma of Classicism," in *Architectural Reflections: Studies in the Philosophy and Practice of Architecture* (London: Butterworth Architecture, 1992), 138–55. Michael Graves used Asplund's Villa Snellman of 1918 as the basis of a studio assignment for first-year architecture students at Princeton in the early seventies. He wanted to redirect attention to the wall and its capacity to reflect space. With the assistance of Caroline Constant and Peter Carl, he wrote an article on the project. See Michael Graves, "The Swedish Connection," *Journal of Architectural Education* 29, no. 1 (1975): 12–13.
5 Quoted in Bann 1998, 184.
6 See the introduction to Chambers 1773.

References

Åhrén, Uno Gunnar Asplund, Wolter Gahn, Sven Markelius, Gregor Paulsson, and Eskil Sundahl. 2008. "Acceptera." In *Modern Swedish Design: Three Founding Texts*, edited by Lucy Creagh, Helena Kåberg, and Barbara Miller Lane, 140–347. New York: Museum of Modern Art.

Andersson, Thorbjörn. 1997. "Appearances and Beyond: Time and Change in Swedish Landscape Architecture." *Journal of Garden History* 17 (4): 278–94.

——. 1998. "The Functionalism of Gardening Art." In *Sweden: Twentieth Century Architecture*, edited by Claes Caldenby, Jöran Lindvall, and Wilfried Wang, 226–41. Munich, Germany: Prestel.

Bann, Stephen. 1998. "Afterword." In *The Landscape Approach*, by Bernard Lassus, 182–92. Philadelphia, PA: University of Pennsylvania Press.

Chambers, William. 1773. *A Dissertation on Oriental Gardening*. Dublin, Ireland: W. Wilson.

Martinson, Harry. 2005. *Views from a Tuft of Grass*. Copenhagen, Denmark: Green Integer.

Strindberg, August. 1998. *Miss Julie and Other Plays*. Oxford: Oxford University Press.

——. 2009. *The Red Room*. Norwich, UK: Norvik Press.

INDEX

Locators in *italics* refer to figures and locators including 'n' refer to notes.